THE BOO

FRENCH
PROVINCIAL
COOKING

T H E   B O O K   O F

FRENCH PROVINCIAL
COOKING

HILAIRE WALDEN

Photographed by
SIMON BUTCHER

HPBooks

ANOTHER BEST SELLING VOLUME FROM HP BOOKS

HPBooks
Published by The Berkley Publishing Group
200 Madison Avenue
New York, NY 10016

9 8 7 6 5 4 3 2 1

ISBN 1-55788-220-7

First Edition ~ December 1995

By arrangement with Salamander Books Ltd.

Home Economist: Justine Dickenson
Printed in Belgium by Proost International Book Production

CONTENTS

INTRODUCTION

French cooking has two facets - that of professional cooking, or *haute cuisine*, and that of the home. *Haute cuisine* is found in restaurants and is emulated the world over. *The Book of French Provincial Cooking*, however, is devoted to the cooking found in people's homes - a cuisine that is strongly regional, richly varied and rooted in tradition. Recipes are passed down from one generation to the next, and early in life all children learn a simple love and respect for good food. Although times are changing, the vast majority of French people still enjoy the same foods they have always eaten, particularly at home. Despite the pressures of modern life good cooking is still appreciated and most people will at least find time to prepare traditional dishes at weekends.

With today's tastes in mind, the best regional recipes from France's rich culinary heritage have been selected for this book. The selection includes the bistro stalwarts Leeks Vinaigrette and Croque Monsieur, rich, slow-simmered Boeuf Bourguignon and Coq au Vin, light and delicate Sole Meunière, sunshine-filled Ratatouille, and classic *pâtisserie* such as Tarte au Citron.

— FRENCH REGIONAL CUISINE —

With three very different coastlines, several neighboring countries and disparate climate and terrain, it is inevitable that local produce, cooking styles and tastes throughout France will reflect these diversities. But even so, certain characteristics are shared by regions with similar environments and climates. For example, simple soups and hearty casseroles feature in colder areas. In areas with lakes and streams, especially in mountainous regions, freshwater fish are popular, while along the coasts sea fish dominate local cuisine. In areas where the climate favors dairy farming, particularly northern France, butter is the fat most commonly used in cooking and many dishes feature cheese and cream, but in the hotter, drier south, which is more suited to the growing of olive trees, olive oil is preferred. It is in the south, too, that garlic comes into its own - contrary to popular belief, garlic is not used everywhere in France.

Although the old provinces of France officially disappeared years ago, they are still known by their traditional names and their local characteristics remain very distinct.

BRITTANY
The rocky coastline of Brittany shelters huge stocks of shellfish such as lobsters, oysters, mussels, clams, scallops and langoustines. Mussels are traditionally cooked as Moules Marinière, or stuffed and broiled. Further out to sea, fishing boats catch sardines, brill, turbot and sea bass.

The interior of Brittany benefits from the benign, warming influence of the Gulf Stream, which makes it possible to grow early vegetables such as artichokes, shallots, baby carrots, cauliflowers, potatoes and garlic. Much of the produce is for canning, freezing or drying. The meat of the sheep that graze on the salt marshes, known as *pré-salé* lamb, has a unique flavor and is a popular delicacy.

Little of Brittany's milk goes into cheese-making (the only well known cheese is Saint-Paulin) but the southern part of the province yields Brittany's famous butter, which is often lightly salted, unlike in the rest of France. Crêpes and galettes, well known Breton dishes, are traditionally made from locally grown buckwheat although sweet ones are now more commonly made from wheat flour.

NORMANDY
The long coastline of Normandy makes this region rich in fine seafood. Dover sole is the prime catch, but the wide variety also includes sardines, mackerel, tuna, bass, turbot, John Dory, mussels, oysters, lobsters, langoustines and crayfish.

On the lush pastures inland graze the cows which produce the regions superb dairy products - rich butter, cream and cheeses such as Camembert, Livarot, Pont l'Evêque and Neufchâtel. Apple orchards are a common sight and many of the apples go to make cider and Calvados (apple brandy), which feature in many local dishes. As in Brittany, the salt marshes nourish delicious *pré-salé* lamb.

PARIS AND THE ILE DE FRANCE
It may be difficult to imagine that this area has a tradition of country cooking, but it was once studded with small villages and market gardens which supplied the rest of the country with vegetables. Crécy is still famed for carrots, the main ingredient in Soupe de Crécy. The towns of Clamart and Saint-Germain are known for their peas and Argenteuil for its asparagus. The region also produces cauliflowers, potatoes, artichokes and onions. Mushrooms (*champignons de Paris*) have been cultivated in the caves and disused quarries around Paris for centuries.

South of Paris, vast expanses of wheat fields provide the flour that upholds the reputation of Parisian bread and *pâtisserie*. Brie, one of the local cheeses, varies considerably in quality, as it may be made in large commercial creameries or by artisans on small farms in one of the 'designated' areas, such as Meaux or Melun.

CHAMPAGNE AND THE NORTH

Although the name of Champagne is often associated with sophistication, the traditional food is typical of other northern areas, with hearty soups, simple stews and dishes based on root vegetables and cabbage. Despite the production of Champagne, the local drink is more often beer than wine, and beer is frequently used for cooking, as in Carbonnade de Boeuf.

Along the coast, fish and shellfish feature in many types of fish stew. Around Dunkirk and Calais, herrings and mackerel are the main catch. Herrings are served smoked and salted, often with a vinaigrette dressing and hot potato salad.

Although much of the region is now heavily industrialized, cereals, sugar beets and hops (for brewing beer) are grown, and commercial farming is an important activity. Vegetables such as cabbage, carrots, leeks, onions and potatoes are dietary staples. On the flat plains, wheat is grown for the thriving flour milling industry. Locally produced cheeses, such as the orange-rinded Maroilles, are often strong flavored and are traditionally eaten with a glass of beer as an accompaniment.

A dish rich in flavor, Cassoulet is a classic example of the cooking of Gascony. There are many versions, but all feature the local ingredients of duck or goose, sausages, garlic and beans.

ALSACE-LORRAINE

Because of their position on the Franco-German border and time spent under the rule of both countries, the cooking of the two northeastern provinces of Alsace and Lorraine exhibits strong similarities to that of Germany. Cold winters also call for hearty, German-style dishes. There is a preponderance of pork, ham, sausages and sauerkraut, which is often served with these meats accompanied by horseradish and mustard. The Alsace city of Strasbourg is an important producer of foie gras.

As the climate is cold and damp, vegetables are limited to cabbage, Brussels sprouts and root vegetables. Tarts and pies, such as the classic Quiche Lorraine, have always been popular, as are sweet tarts made from fruits including the cherries from the sheltered valleys of Lorraine. Among the large range of popular cakes are Madeleines, originally from Lorraine. Local cheeses, such as Munster, are strong flavored and pungent.

FRANCHE-COMTE AND THE ALPS

Peaks and valleys, lakes and streams make this a beautiful area. The lakes and rivers are celebrated for trout, Arctic char, grayling, pike and crayfish. Game is found in the mountains and wild mushrooms in the woods and pastures. As in other mountain areas, hams and sausages are dried in the clear, crisp mountain air. In the valleys grow fine fruits including peaches and apricots.

The dairy products of this area are exceptional, flavored by the aromatic plants in the cattle pastures. The principal cheeses are Gruyère and Emmentaler (although both originally from Switzerland) as well as Beaufort, Reblochon and Tomme de Savoie, many of which feature in local dishes such as Gratin Savoyarde. In the south of the province, Dauphiné is France's largest producer of walnuts. Due to its proximity to both Provence and the Alps, Dauphinoise cuisine features olive oil as well as butter and cream.

BURGUNDY AND LYONNAIS

With the best available natural resources to maintain its gastronomic reputation, the cooking of Burgundy is rich and varied. Large Charolais cattle provide lean meat that is ideally suited to the long, slow braising of dishes such as Boeuf Bourguignon, Bresse produces the famed chickens, *poulet de Bresse*, while the local countryside provides game, mushrooms, snails and river fish such as trout.

The key ingredient in Burgundian cooking is wine. White wine goes into the region's fish stews and ham and chicken dishes. Red wine is used in the cooking of nearly all meat and game dishes, and sometimes poultry as in Coq au Vin. The selection of cheese is wide, although only a few, such as Epoisses and Charolles, are well known, as they are usually produced on a small scale for local consumption.

Known as the 'temple of gastronomy', Lyon is the center of an enormous *charcuterie*, or meat curing,

industry, with a range of products which are enjoyed throughout France and exported internationally. Onions are a hallmark of local cooking, widely used in Lyonnais dishes. The Lyonnais also have a love of chocolate, first encouraged by *confiseurs* from Italy in the 18th century.

PROVENCE AND LANGUEDOC-ROUSSILLON

The food of these Mediterranean provinces is colorful and richly aromatic, heady with garlic and olive oil and fragrant with herbs. Fish specific to the Mediterranean feature strongly in local cooking. Anchovies for example, form the basis of Anchoïade (Anchovy Spread). Of the larger fish, the most plentiful are sardines, sea bream, red mullet and sea bass, all of which are frequently charcoal-grilled.

Almost every variety of sun-loving fruit and vegetable is grown. Flavorful tomatoes, eggplant, zucchini and sweet peppers feature in local specialties such as Ratatouille, slowly cooked until almost melted (one of the secrets of Provençal cooking). Local fruits include cherries, peaches, nectarines, melons, apricots, strawberries, figs and pears, sold fresh or preserved as jam or crystallized fruit. At the eastern end of the region, an Italian influence can be detected in dishes such as Pissaladière, more like pizza than quiche. Towards the Pyrenees, pork dishes and pork products become more common, and a Spanish influence is apparent.

THE PYRENEES

On the western coast of this province lies the Basque country. Flame red is the Basque color - from their tiled roofs to their traditional berets - and it is also the color of their cooking, which is dominated by tomatoes and peppers. Basque cuisine relies largely on such fish as tuna, swordfish, sardines and anchovies. Sea salt is used to preserve anchovies and cod, as well as the famed ham, *jambon de Bayonne*.

The emphasis is on hearty, simple soups and stews, and from the days when meat was an expensive luxury, many dishes are based on cornmeal, as is Italian polenta. At the eastern end of the Pyrenees, food is influenced by the Mediterranean.

GASCONY
The food of Gascony is simple and rich - goose, duck, pork and foie gras form the basis of the diet and appear in many soups and stews, of which the best known is Cassoulet. Goose or duck fat are used for cooking in place of butter or oil. Garlic (which some now believe has helped protect Gascons against heart disease their diet could cause) is used generously, often whole cloves rather than chopped. When cooked gently and slowly, as in Garlic Chicken, the flavor becomes mellow and mild. Many fruits grow in the area, and the plump, shiny black prunes of Agen are reputed to be the best in the world. Milk, butter and cheese used to be rare commodities and cattle were used solely for ploughing. Even goat milk and cheese have become popular only in the last 25 years.

THE WEST
Bordeaux, the major city of western France, is better known for its great wines than its food, which is generally quite plain. One renowned dish, however, is Entrecôte Bordelaise. Further north in Charente, the lush pastures are ideal for dairy farming and Charantais butter is highly prized. Charente also produces the renowned brandy, Cognac.

The proximity of the rich Atlantic coastline is reflected in the number of fish dishes. Oysters, mussels and clams are farmed along the coast and the most popular fish are sole, sardines (sometimes eaten raw with sea salt and bread and butter) skate, grey mullet, sea bream, whiting and monkfish.

The climate is very favorable for spring vegetables and fruit. Orchards and hedgerows yield blackberries, plums, apples, pears, chestnuts and walnuts, all of which may be preserved or made into fruit brandies and liqueurs. Périgord, one of the best known culinary areas of France, has a worldwide reputation for foie gras and for truffles, and the practice of using pigs to sniff out this rare underground fungus continues to this day.

THE CENTER
The heart of this region is the Massif Central, a remote, rugged area where the cooking is simple and substantial, designed to provide warmth and energy at little cost. Staple foods are root vegetables, cabbage and bread. Chestnuts, wild mushrooms, sausages, pork, ham and bacon feature strongly. On the slopes of the valleys that catch the summer sun, and in the provinces of Limousin and Bourbonnais, fruits are grown for pies, tarts and desserts, Clafoutis being a regional favorite.

The pride of the region is its cheeses, made from the milk of cows that graze on lush, herb-strewn pastures. The large variety includes Cantal and Saint-Nectaire as well as blue cheeses such as Bleu d'Auvergne.

THE LOIRE
This area has been known as the 'garden of France' for many years. Although the cooking is simple, the excellence of the produce lends it distinction. There are many early vegetables such as carrots, artichokes, asparagus, salad greens and potatoes. There is also an abundance of apples and pears, peaches, apricots, melons, strawberries and black currants, often used in desserts. Fruit tarts are a specialty, and Tarte Tatin, an upside-down apple pie, is probably the best known. The area around Tours is famous for dishes made with prunes.

As the area is centered on a river, as well as being near the sea, fish is a cornerstone of the cuisine. The Loire does not provide as much fish as previously, but stocks are building up again. Popular meats are poultry, pork and pork products, such as rillettes. Cheeses are made from goat milk and on a small scale, the best known are Sainte-Maure and Valençay.

The local wines - red, white and sparkling, sweet and dry - are used to good effect in regional specialities such as Salmon in Red Wine, an unusual combination that is successful because of the softness of the red wines.

VICHYSSOISE

3 tablespoons butter
6 leeks, white parts only, sliced
10 oz. baking potatoes, diced
2-1/2 cups chicken or vegetable stock
1-1/4 cups milk
1/3 cup whipping cream
Salt and freshly ground pepper
Chopped fresh chives, to garnish

Melt butter in a saucepan, add leeks and potatoes and stir to coat with butter. Cover and cook over low heat, stirring occasionally, 5 minutes or until beginning to soften.

Add stock and bring to a boil. Reduce heat, cover and simmer 15 to 20 minutes or until vegetables are tender.

Stir in milk, then press mixture through a strainer. Let cool, then stir in cream, salt and pepper. Cover and refrigerate until chilled thoroughly, at least 2 hours. Garnish with chives and serve in chilled bowls.

Makes 4 servings.

WATERCRESS SOUP

2 tablespoons butter
1 onion, chopped
8 oz. potatoes, diced
2-1/2 cups chicken, veal or vegetable stock
2 bunches watercress, chopped
About 1-1/4 cups milk
Pinch of freshly grated nutmeg
Salt and freshly ground pepper
Fresh chives, to garnish

Melt butter in a saucepan, add onion and cook over low heat, stirring occasionally, 5 minutes or until soft. Add potatoes.

Stir in stock, bring to a boil, reduce heat and simmer 15 minutes or until potatoes are tender. Add watercress and simmer 30 seconds. Transfer to a blender or food processor and process very briefly (otherwise it will become 'gluey'). Press through a strainer and return soup to rinsed-out pan.

Stir in enough milk to give desired consistency. Add nutmeg, salt and pepper and reheat gently without boiling. Garnish with chives and serve.

Makes 4 servings.

Note: For best results, use whole milk.

LENTIL SOUP

2 tablespoons olive oil
1 onion, chopped
2 garlic cloves, chopped
2 slices thick-cut bacon, diced
1 leek, sliced
2 carrots, diced
1 stalk celery, sliced
3/4 cup green or brown lentils
1-3/4 cups tomato sauce
1/4 cup chopped fresh herbs such as parsley,
   tarragon, thyme and marjoram
1 bay leaf
Salt and freshly ground pepper
Chopped fresh parsley and croûtons, to garnish

Heat oil in a saucepan. Add onion, garlic and bacon and cook, stirring occasionally, 4 or 5 minutes. Stir in vegetables, lentils, tomato sauce, chopped herbs, bay leaf and 3-3/4 cups water.

Bring to a boil, reduce heat and simmer 25 minutes or until vegetables and lentils are tender. Season with salt and pepper, garnish with chopped parsley and croûtons and serve.

Makes 4 servings.

-CREAMED CAULIFLOWER SOUP-

1 cauliflower, divided into flowerets
6 green onions, cut into 1-inch lengths
1 bay leaf
3/4 cup sliced almonds
3-3/4 cups vegetable, chicken or veal stock
1 cup milk
Salt and freshly ground pepper

Cook cauliflower, green onions, bay leaf and half the almonds in 2-1/2 cups of the stock 10 to 15 minutes or until cauliflower is tender.

Preheat broiler. Spread remaining almonds in a single layer on a baking sheet and toast, turning occasionally, until lightly browned.

Remove bay leaf from soup and purée soup in a blender or food processor. Return to rinsed-out pan, add remaining stock, bring to a boil and boil 3 minutes. Reduce heat and stir in milk. Reheat gently without boiling and season with salt and pepper. Sprinkle with toasted almonds and serve.

Makes 4 servings.

HERBED PEA SOUP

1/4 cup unsalted butter
1 leek, finely chopped
1 small head butter lettuce, separated into leaves
About 3-3/4 cups vegetable or chicken stock or water
Several sprigs of chervil
Few sprigs of parsley
1 lb. fresh or frozen green peas
Salt and freshly ground pepper
Half-and-half, to garnish

Melt butter in a saucepan, add leek and cook, stirring occasionally, 5 minutes or until soft. Add lettuce and cook 1 or 2 minutes or until leaves have wilted.

Add stock or water, chervil, parsley and peas. Bring to a boil, reduce heat and simmer 10 minutes if using fresh peas. If using frozen peas, simmer 5 minutes or until peas are tender.

Purée soup in a blender or food processor and return to rinsed-out pan. Add salt and pepper and reheat gently without boiling. If soup is too thick, add some boiling stock or water. Swirl in half-and-half and serve.

Makes 4 servings.

SOUPE DE CRÉCY

1/4 cup butter
1-1/4 lbs. small carrots, sliced
2 leeks, chopped
6 oz. baking potatoes, diced
Leaves from 2 sprigs of tarragon, chopped
3-3/4 cup boiling water
Salt and freshly ground pepper
Tarragon leaves, to garnish

Melt 3 tablespoons of the butter in a saucepan, add carrots and leeks and stir to coat with butter. Add potatoes, cover and cook over low heat, stirring occasionally, 5 minutes or until beginning to soften.

Add tarragon, boiling water, salt and pepper. Bring to a boil, reduce heat, cover and simmer 25 minutes or until vegetables are very tender.

Allow soup to cool slightly, then press through a strainer or purée in a blender or food processor. Return to rinsed-out pan and reheat gently without boiling. Add a piece of the remaining butter to each serving, garnish with tarragon leaves and serve.

Makes 4 servings.

ONION SOUP

1/3 cup butter
1-1/2 lbs. large onions, thinly sliced
4-1/2 cups beef stock
1-1/4 cups dry white wine
Large pinch of mixed dried herbs
Pinch of freshly grated nutmeg
Salt and freshly ground pepper
6 slices French bread
5 oz. (1-1/4 cups) shredded Gruyère cheese
Flat-leaf parsley sprigs, to garnish

Melt butter in a large, heavy saucepan, add onions, stir to coat with the butter and lay a piece of waxed paper on top.

Cook over very low heat, without stirring, 20 to 30 minutes or until onions are soft and rich golden brown. Add stock, wine, dried herbs, nutmeg, salt and pepper and bring to a boil. Reduce heat, cover and simmer 45 minutes. Meanwhile, preheat oven to 350F (180C). Arrange bread slices on a baking sheet and bake 10 to 15 minutes or until dried but not browned.

Preheat broiler. Divide soup among heatproof soup bowls. Float a slice of bread on top and sprinkle with cheese. Broil until cheese is bubbling and golden. Garnish with flat-leaf parsley sprigs and serve immediately.

Makes 6 servings.

SOUPE AU PISTOU

1/2 cup dried haricot beans, soaked overnight
1 onion, finely chopped
5 oz. pumpkin, chopped (optional)
1 stalk celery, sliced
2 small leeks, chopped
2 baby turnips, diced
6 oz. small green beans, cut into 1-inch pieces
5 oz. shelled broad beans or lima beans (about 1 cup)
3 ripe tomatoes, peeled and chopped
2 oz. fine vermicelli
Salt and freshly ground pepper
PISTOU:
Handful of basil leaves
3 garlic cloves
6 tablespoons olive oil
3/4 cup grated Parmesan cheese

Drain haricot beans. Put into a large saucepan with onion, pumpkin, if using, and 7-1/2 cups water. Bring to a boil and boil rapidly 10 minutes. Cover and simmer 1 hour. Add celery, leeks and turnips and cook 10 to 15 minutes. Add remaining ingredients. Cook 10 minutes or until beans and vegetables are tender.

Meanwhile, make the pistou. Coarsely chop basil. Using a pestle and mortar, pound garlic with the basil, then gradually add oil, stirring until well blended. Stir in Parmesan cheese and 1 or 2 tablespoons of hot soup. Pour the soup into warmed bowls, spoon a little pistou into each serving, garnish with Parmesan shavings and serve.

Makes 6 servings.

— MEDITERRANEAN FISH SOUP —

1/4 cup olive oil
1 large onion, finely chopped
2 garlic cloves, crushed
1 small fennel bulb, chopped
2 lbs. mixed fish and shellfish
2 tomatoes, peeled and chopped
Several parsley sprigs, chopped
3 sprigs each thyme and basil
Pinch of saffron strands
Strip of orange peel
Salt and freshly ground pepper
About 4-1/2 cups fish stock

Heat oil in a saucepan, add onion, garlic and fennel and cook 5 minutes or until soft.

Cut fish into 1-1/2-inch pieces. Add tomatoes, herbs, saffron, orange peel, salt and pepper to saucepan. Lay fish on top and add just enough stock to cover fish. Bring to barely simmering and cook over low heat, uncovered, 8 minutes.

Add shellfish and cook 5 minutes or until fish and shellfish are tender. Skim any scum from surface of soup and serve.

Makes 4 to 6 servings.

Note: For best results use a selection of white fish such as haddock, cod or whiting. Don't use oily fish such as mackerel as it gives a bitter taste to the soup.

ASPARAGUS HOLLANDAISE

2 lbs. asparagus, trimmed
Salt and freshly ground pepper
HOLLANDAISE SAUCE:
3 egg yolks
3/4 cup unsalted butter
1-3/4 tablespoons lemon juice
2 teaspoons water
Strips of lemon zest, to garnish

Tie asparagus into 4 bundles with string. Pour enough water into a deep saucepan to come 1-1/2 to 2-inches up asparagus stems. Bring to a boil.

Add asparagus and salt and cover tightly with a lid or piece of foil. Reduce heat and simmer 6 to 8 minutes or until asparagus stems are tender. Lift out asparagus, cut string and drain asparagus on paper towels. Transfer to warmed serving plates and keep warm.

Meanwhile, make hollandaise sauce. Put egg yolks into a blender or food processor. Gently heat butter until hot. Put lemon juice and water into a small saucepan and bring to a boil. Turn motor to slow speed and trickle lemon juice mixture onto egg yolks. With motor still running, slowly trickle in butter, adding all except white sediment, until sauce is thick and creamy. Season with salt and pepper and pour over asparagus. Garnish and serve immediately.

Makes 6 servings.

LEEKS VINAIGRETTE

12 small leeks, white parts only
1-1/2 tablespoons chopped fresh parsley
1 hard-cooked egg, chopped
Dill sprigs and red bell pepper strips, to garnish
VINAIGRETTE:
1 tablespoon white wine vinegar
1/2 teaspoon Dijon mustard
Salt and freshly ground pepper
4 or 5 tablespoons olive oil

Arrange leeks in a steamer, cover and steam 6 to 10 minutes or until tender. Drain on paper towels.

To make vinaigrette, whisk together vinegar, mustard, salt and pepper. Slowly add oil, whisking constantly. Transfer leeks to serving plates, add vinaigrette and let cool slightly. Sprinkle leeks with parsley and egg, garnish with dill sprigs and bell pepper strips and serve.

Makes 4 servings.

— MUSHROOMS À LA GRECQUE —

2 tablespoons olive oil
1 onion, finely chopped
1 garlic clove, chopped
1 tablespoon coriander seeds
1-1/4 cups red wine
1 tablespoon tomato paste
Bouquet garni
1 lb. button mushrooms
1-1/4 lbs. ripe tomatoes, peeled, seeded and
   chopped
Salt and freshly ground pepper
Flat-leaf parsley sprigs, to garnish

Heat oil in a large skillet, add onion and garlic and cook, stirring occasionally, 7 minutes or until beginning to color.

Stir in coriander seeds, wine, tomato paste and bouquet garni. Add mushrooms, tomatoes, salt and pepper.

Bring to a boil, reduce heat and simmer 10 minutes or until mushrooms are just tender. Transfer to a bowl and let cool. Cover and refrigerate for several hours. Remove bouquet garni. Garnish with flat-leaf parsley and serve.

Makes 4 servings.

Note: A bouquet garni is a bunch of fresh herbs used to flavor a dish but removed before serving. The herbs may vary but it always includes parsley, thyme and a bay leaf.

CELERIAC RÉMOULADE

2/3 cup mayonnaise
2 or 3 teaspoons Dijon mustard
1 teaspoon fresh lemon juice
Salt and freshly ground pepper
1 lb. celeriac
2 tablespoons chopped fresh chervil or parsley
Lettuce leaves, to serve

Put mayonnaise into a large bowl, add mustard and lemon juice to taste and season with salt and pepper. Peel and coarsely grate celeriac.

Add celeriac to a large saucepan of boiling water and cook 30 to 60 seconds. Drain celeriac and rinse under cold running water. Drain again and dry on paper towels.

Mix celeriac into mayonnaise. Spoon into lettuce leaves. Sprinkle with chervil or parsley and serve.

Makes 4 servings.

Variation: Celeriac tastes better if briefly blanched in this way, but it can also be eaten raw.

—— BELL PEPPER VINAIGRETTE ——

4 red bell peppers
4 hard-cooked eggs, halved
1 (2-oz.) can anchovies in olive oil, drained
2 tablespoons capers
2 tablespoons chopped fresh flat-leaf parsley
VINAIGRETTE:
2-1/2 tablespoons red wine vinegar
1/2 cup olive oil
Salt and freshly ground pepper

Preheat broiler. Place whole bell peppers on broiler rack and broil, turning occasionally, until charred and blistered all over.

Leave until cool enough to handle, then peel, working over a bowl to catch the juices. Cut bell peppers in half and discard cores and seeds. Arrange bell pepper halves on serving plates and add juices from bowl.

To make vinaigrette, whisk together vinegar, oil, salt and pepper and pour over bell peppers. Remove egg yolks from whites. Chop egg whites and scatter over bell peppers. Arrange anchovies on top and sprinkle with capers. Press egg yolks through a strainer over bell peppers, sprinkle with chopped flat-leaf parsley and serve.

Makes 4 servings.

TAPÉNADE

7 oz. small ripe olives, pitted
2 oz. capers
4 anchovy fillets
1 or 2 garlic cloves, crushed
1 tablespoon Dijon mustard
1/2 cup olive oil
1 teaspoon chopped fresh thyme
1/2 to 1 teaspoon fresh lemon juice
Freshly ground pepper
8 slices French bread
Chopped fresh chives, to garnish

Using a pestle and mortar, pound olives, capers, anchovies, garlic and mustard to a smooth paste.

Work in a little oil, a drop at a time, then gradually add remaining oil, pounding constantly. Stir in thyme, lemon juice and pepper to taste. If necessary, adjust the consistency by adding more oil (it should be a thick, spreadable paste).

Toast bread on both sides. Spread with tapénade, garnish with chopped chives and serve.

Makes 4 to 6 servings.

Note: Tapénade can be kept in a covered container in the refrigerator for several weeks. Serve at room temperature.

ANCHOVY SPREAD

2 garlic cloves, crushed
2 (2-oz.) cans anchovies in olive oil, drained
1-1/2 tablespoons chopped fresh basil
1/3 cup olive oil
2 or 3 teaspoons red wine vinegar
2 teaspoons tomato paste
Freshly ground pepper

Using a pestle and mortar, pound garlic and anchovies to form a smooth paste.

Pound in basil. Work in a little oil, a drop at a time, then gradually add remaining oil, pounding constantly.

Stir in vinegar and tomato paste and season with pepper. Serve with crudités and country bread.

Makes 4 to 6 servings.

Note: Anchovy spread can be stored in the refrigerator in a glass jar. Stir and adjust the level of vinegar and basil to taste before serving.

— CREAM CHEESE WITH HERBS —

8 oz. well-drained fromage blanc or low-fat cream
  cheese
1 tablespoon chopped fresh parsley
1 tablespoon chopped fresh chives
1 tablespoon finely chopped shallot
1 tablespoon olive oil
2 tablespoons dry white wine
1 teaspoon white wine vinegar (optional)
Salt and freshly ground pepper
1/4 cup crème fraîche or whipping cream
Parsley sprigs and fresh chives, to garnish

Beat cheese 2 or 3 minutes to lighten it. Beat
in parsley, chives, shallot, oil, wine, vinegar,
if using, and salt and pepper.

Lightly beat crème fraîche or cream and fold
into cheese mixture. Spoon into serving
bowl, cover and refrigerate. Garnish with
parsley sprigs and chives and serve with
crudités.

Makes 4 servings.

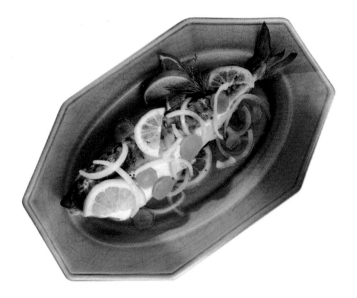

— MACKEREL IN WHITE WINE —

6 small mackerel, cleaned and heads removed
Salt and freshly ground pepper
1 lemon, sliced
1 small carrot, thinly sliced
1 onion, thinly sliced
1/2 to 1 fresh red chile
12 coriander seeds
2 whole cloves
Bouquet garni
1/3 cup white wine vinegar
About 1-1/4 cups dry white wine
Lime wedges and dill sprigs, to garnish

Season fish with salt and pepper and lay them in a nonmetallic flameproof dish. Cover with lemon slices and vegetables, then add spices. Add bouquet garni, vinegar and enough wine to just cover. Cover and let stand 20 minutes.

Heat dish gently to simmering point. Immediately remove from heat and let cool. Discard bouquet garni and chile. Arrange on serving plates, spoon vegetables and juices over fish, garnish with lime wedges and dill sprigs and serve.

Makes 6 servings.

Note: The flavor of the mackerel will improve if kept in the refrigerator, covered, for a few days.

— SAUTÉED CHICKEN LIVERS —

1/4 cup unsalted butter
2 tablespoons finely chopped shallot
8 oz. chicken livers, trimmed
1/3 cup dry white wine
4 oz. seedless green grapes, halved
Salt and freshly ground pepper
Lemon juice (optional)
Chopped fresh thyme or tarragon, to garnish

Melt butter in a large skillet, add chopped shallot and cook, stirring occasionally, 3 minutes or until soft.

Add chicken livers and cook quickly, stirring, 1 to 1-1/2 minutes or until crisp on outside and still pink in center. Remove with a slotted spoon, cover and keep warm.

Stir wine into pan, dislodging browned bits, and boil until slightly reduced. Reduce heat, add grapes and simmer to warm through. Return chicken livers to pan with any juices. Add salt and pepper and a squeeze of lemon juice, if needed. Sprinkle with chopped thyme or tarragon and serve.

Makes 2 servings.

PÂTÉ DE CAMPAGNE

12 oz. veal or chicken, finely chopped
1-1/2 lbs. lean unsmoked bacon, finely chopped
8 oz. calf or lamb liver, finely chopped
2 tablespoons butter
2 small onions, finely chopped
10 oz. ham, chopped
3 or 4 garlic cloves, finely chopped
2 tablespoons chopped fresh parsley
2 teaspoons herbes de Provence
2 teaspoons freshly ground pepper
2 teaspoons salt
1/2 teaspoon ground allspice
1/2 cup dry white wine
2 tablespoons brandy

Put veal or chicken, bacon and liver into a bowl. Melt butter in a saucepan and cook onions, stirring occasionally, 7 minutes or until lightly browned. Add onions to meats with all remaining ingredients and mix well. Cover and refrigerate 2 hours. Preheat oven to 325F (165C).

Pack pâté mixture into a 7-1/2-cup terrine. Cover with foil. Put into a roasting pan and pour in enough boiling water to come three-quarters of the way up sides of terrine. Bake 1-1/2 hours. To test if cooked, insert a skewer in center and count to 5. If skewer feels hot when withdrawn, the pâté is cooked. Remove from roasting pan and let cool. Put weights on top and refrigerate for a few hours. Turn out, slice and serve.

Makes 10 to 12 servings.

PISSALADIÈRE

1/4 cup olive oil, plus extra for brushing
2 lbs. Spanish onions, thinly sliced
1 large garlic clove, crushed
Salt and freshly ground pepper
1 (2-oz.) can anchovies in olive oil
12 large pitted ripe olives, halved
1 teaspoon herbes de Provence
Basil sprigs, to garnish
CRUST:
2 cups bread flour
1 teaspoon herbes de Provence
1 teaspoon fast-acting yeast
1 teaspoon salt

Heat oil in a large, heavy skillet, add onions, garlic, salt and pepper and cook gently, stirring occasionally, 25 to 30 minutes, until onions are soft and golden. Let cool.

Meanwhile, make crust. Stir together flour, herbs, yeast, salt and pepper. Slowly stir in about 3/4 cup warm water (105F, 40C) to make a smooth dough.

Turn dough out on a lightly floured surface and knead until firm and elastic. Lightly oil a 13- x 9-inch baking pan. Roll out dough to fit pan and put into pan, pushing dough up sides and into corners.

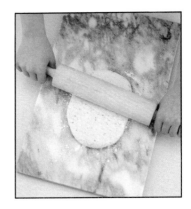

Brush dough with oil, cover and let rise 30 minutes or until dough is lightly puffy. Preheat oven to 425F (220C).

Spread onions over dough. Drain anchovies, reserving oil. Cut anchovies lengthwise in half and arrange in lattice pattern on top of onions. Arrange olives on top, sprinkle with herbs and drizzle with anchovy oil. Bake on top shelf of oven 20 to 25 minutes. Cut into squares, garnish with basil sprigs and serve warm or room temperature.

Makes 4 to 6 servings.

LEEK TART

1/4 cup butter
4 leeks, halved lengthwise and thinly sliced
Salt and freshly ground pepper
4 egg yolks
1 cup milk or half-and-half
Leaves from 4 sprigs of tarragon, finely chopped
3 tablespoons freshly grated Parmesan cheese
   (optional)
PASTRY:
1-1/2 cups all-purpose flour
1/3 cup butter, chilled, diced
1 egg yolk

Melt butter in a large saucepan, add leeks, salt and pepper and cook over low heat, stirring occasionally, 10 minutes or until soft.

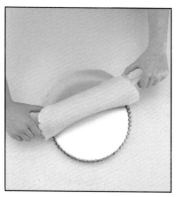

Leave leeks to cool. To make pastry, mix together flour, salt and pepper. Add butter and cut in until mixture resembles fine bread crumbs. Stir in egg yolk and enough cold water to make a firm but not dry dough. Cover and refrigerate 30 minutes. Thinly roll out pastry on a lightly floured surface and line an 8-inch tart pan. Prick bottom with a fork and line with foil. Fill with dried beans and refrigerate 20 minutes. Preheat oven to 400F (205C).

Bake pastry 10 minutes. Remove beans and foil and bake another 10 minutes. Reduce oven temperature to 350F (180C). Mix together egg yolks, milk or half-and-half, tarragon, salt and pepper and Parmesan cheese, if using. Arrange leeks in pastry and add egg mixture. Bake 30 to 40 minutes or until lightly set and golden. Serve warm or cold with a salad.

Makes 4 to 6 servings.

PAN BAGNA

1 loaf French bread, cut crosswise into 4
1-1/2 tablespoons white wine vinegar
1 teaspoon Dijon mustard
5 tablespoons olive oil
2 garlic cloves, crushed
Salt and freshly ground pepper
8 crisp lettuce leaves
4 beefsteak tomatoes, sliced
4 green onions, thinly sliced
1 red bell pepper, peeled (page 25) and sliced
1/2 cucumber, sliced
12 basil leaves
16 pitted ripe olives
1 (2-oz.) can anchovies in olive oil, drained and
  quartered

Slice each piece of bread lengthwise in half
and pull out most of the soft bread from
inside. Whisk together vinegar, mustard, oil,
garlic, salt and pepper. Brush a little over
inside of pieces of bread.

Cover bottom halves of bread with half the
lettuce. Arrange tomatoes, green onions, bell
pepper, cucumber, basil, olives and
anchovies on top. Drizzle with remaining
dressing, add remaining lettuce and cover
with the top halves of bread. Cover with a
board, put heavy weights on top and set aside
2 hours. Cut each piece in half, garnish with
basil sprigs and ripe olives and serve.

Makes 4 servings.

CROQUE MONSIEUR

8 slices firm white bread
Unsalted butter, softened
4 oz. (1 cup) shredded Gruyère cheese
4 slices cooked ham
Dijon mustard
Salad greens and parsley sprigs, to garnish

Preheat broiler. Butter one side of each bread slice. Sprinkle half the cheese over buttered sides of four slices, top each with a slice of ham and spread ham with a little mustard.

Cover ham with remaining cheese, then put remaining bread on top, buttered side down, and press together. Broil sandwiches on both sides until bread is toasted and cheese melted. Cut in half, garnish with salad greens and parsley sprigs and serve hot.

Makes 2 to 4 servings.

EGGS IN RED WINE

1/4 cup butter
4 oz. mushrooms, chopped
1 small onion, chopped
1-1/4 cups red wine
3/4 cup vegetable or chicken stock
1 tarragon sprig
4 eggs
Salt and freshly ground pepper
4 slices country bread, toasted
Chopped fresh parsley and marjoram sprigs, to
  garnish

Melt half the butter in a heavy saucepan. Add mushrooms and onion and cook over low heat, stirring occasionally, 5 minutes or until soft.

Add wine, stock and tarragon. Bring to a boil, reduce heat and simmer 10 minutes. Discard tarragon sprig. Remove vegetables with a slotted spoon and keep warm. Heat cooking liquid just barely to a simmer. Carefully break in eggs and poach 2 or 3 minutes. Remove with a slotted spoon, drain on paper towels and keep warm.

Boil liquid until slightly syrupy. Reduce heat and whisk in remaining butter, a small piece at a time. Season with salt and pepper. Butter the toasted bread and top with vegetables. Place eggs on top, add sauce, garnish with parsley and marjoram and serve.

Makes 4 servings.

Variation: This dish can be made with white wine instead of red, if you prefer.

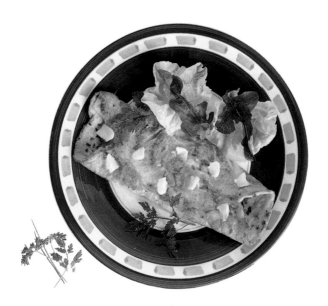

OMELETTE AUX HERBES

1 tablespoon mixed chopped fresh parsley, tarragon, chives and chervil
Salt and freshly ground pepper
3 eggs, very lightly beaten
2 tablespoons unsalted butter
Chervil sprigs, to garnish
Salad greens, to serve

Add half the herbs, salt and pepper to eggs. Heat half the butter in a 9- or 10-inch skillet. Pour eggs into skillet and cook over medium heat, stirring gently with a fork or spatula and drawing egg from the sides of pan as it sets, to allow the liquid egg to flow to the sides.

Stop stirring when egg is just set underneath and still slightly liquid on top. Sprinkle with remaining herbs and cook 30 to 60 seconds.

Using a spatula, flip over one-third of omelette, then flip over the other side, to fold sides over center. Roll out of pan onto a warmed plate. Dot with remaining butter, garnish with chervil sprigs and serve with salad greens.

Makes 1 serving.

PIPÉRADE

4 thin slices Bayonne ham or prosciutto
1-1/2 tablespoons olive oil
1 Spanish onion, chopped
2 garlic cloves, chopped
1 green bell pepper, thinly sliced
1 red bell pepper, thinly sliced
1-1/2 lbs. very ripe tomatoes, peeled, seeded and
    chopped
Salt and freshly ground pepper
6 to 8 eggs, beaten
Parsley sprigs and chopped fresh parsley, to garnish

Trim fat from ham. Dice fat and heat with oil in a heavy skillet until fat melts. Add onion and garlic.

Cook, stirring occasionally, 5 minutes or until soft. Add bell peppers, tomatoes, salt and pepper and simmer 15 minutes, stirring occasionally, until lightly thickened. Transfer two-thirds of vegetables to another pan, cover and keep warm. Put ham under a slow broiler to warm.

Stir eggs into remaining vegetables and cook over low heat, stirring gently, until eggs begin to thicken. Immediately remove from heat. Put ham on warmed serving plates, top with vegetable mixture and then egg mixture. Garnish with parsley and serve immediately.

Makes 4 servings.

GOUGÈRES

1/2 cup butter, diced
Scant cup of water
1-1/4 cups all-purpose flour, sifted
3 or 4 eggs, beaten
1 cup finely grated Emmentaler cheese
Cayenne pepper
Salt and freshly ground pepper
Beaten egg or milk for glazing
Flat-leaf parsley sprigs, to garnish

Preheat oven to 400F (205C). Put butter into a saucepan with water and heat until melted, then bring quickly to a boil. Remove from heat and quickly stir in flour.

Return to low heat and stir until mixture comes away from side of pan and looks shiny. Remove from heat and stir about 1 minute, until cooled, then gradually beat in three-quarters of the beaten eggs, until mixture is smooth. Add more egg as required until mixture is glossy and soft, but not runny. Beat in 3/4 cup cheese, cayenne, salt and pepper.

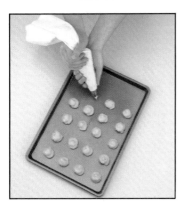

Lightly butter 2 baking sheets. Spoon mixture into a pastry bag fitted with a 1/2-inch plain tip. Pipe 48 small balls on to baking sheets, spacing them 1 inch apart. Brush with beaten egg or milk, sprinkle with remaining cheese and bake 15 minutes or until puffed, crisp and golden. Garnish with flat-leaf parsley and serve immediately.

Makes 6 to 8 servings.

MUSSELS WITH CREAM

1-1/2 cups dry white wine
Bouquet garni
4 lbs. mussels, scrubbed and trimmed
1/4 cup butter
1 onion, chopped
1/2 teaspoon curry powder
1-1/2 tablespoons all-purpose flour
2/3 cup crème fraîche or whipping cream
Salt and freshly ground pepper
Flat-leaf parsley sprigs, to garnish

Put wine, bouquet garni and mussels in a large saucepan and bring to a boil.

Cover tightly and cook over high heat 4 minutes, shaking pan occasionally, until mussels open. Discard any mussels that remain closed. Remove mussels from shells, pouring their liquor back into pan and discarding shells. Put mussels into a bowl, cover and keep warm. Boil cooking liquid until reduced by half.

Melt butter in a saucepan, add onion and cook, stirring occasionally, 5 minutes or until soft. Add curry powder and flour and cook, stirring, 1-1/2 minutes. Strain cooking liquid and slowly stir into onion mixture. Bring to a boil, stirring, then simmer 4 minutes. Stir in crème fraîche or cream, salt and pepper and boil until lightly thickened. Stir in mussels, garnish with flat-leaf parsley and serve.

Makes 4 servings.

STUFFED MUSSELS

4 lbs. mussels, scrubbed and trimmed
3 thyme sprigs
HERB BUTTER STUFFING:
1 shallot, finely chopped
2 garlic cloves, finely chopped
1 tablespoon finely chopped fresh parsley
1 tablespoon finely chopped fresh chives
1 teaspoon chopped fresh chervil
1 cup fresh bread crumbs
2/3 cup butter, softened
1 to 1-1/2 tablespoons fresh lemon juice
Salt and freshly ground pepper
Flat-leaf parsley sprigs, to garnish

To make herb butter stuffing, mix together shallot, garlic, herbs and bread crumbs, then beat into butter. Add lemon juice, salt and pepper and set aside. Cover the bottoms of shallow ovenproof serving dishes with a thick layer of coarse sea salt or crumpled foil. Pour 1-1/4 cups water into a large saucepan. Bring to a boil, add mussels and thyme, cover tightly and cook over high heat, 4 minutes, shaking occasionally, until mussels open.

Preheat oven to 450F (230C). Drain mussels, discarding any that remain closed. Discard top shells of mussels and arrange mussels in dishes on top of salt or foil. Divide herb butter among mussels and bake 10 to 12 minutes or until sizzling and golden. Garnish with flat-leaf parsley and serve at once.

Makes 4 to 6 servings.

MOULES MARINIÈRE

2 tablespoons unsalted butter
2 shallots, finely chopped
2 garlic cloves, finely chopped
1 cup dry white wine
Bouquet garni, including parsley, thyme and chives
Freshly ground pepper
2 lbs. mussels, scrubbed and trimmed
3 or 4 tablespoons mixed chopped fresh herbs such
　　as tarragon, chives, parsley and fennel
Lemon juice (optional)

Melt butter in a large saucepan, add shallots
and garlic and cook, stirring occasionally, 2
minutes or until soft.

Add wine, bouquet garni and pepper and
bring to a boil. Add mussels, cover tightly
and cook over high heat 4 minutes, shaking
pan occasionally, until mussels have opened.
Discard any mussels that remain closed.

Remove mussels with a slotted spoon,
transfer to warmed large soup plates and
keep warm. Discard bouquet garni. Add
chopped herbs and lemon juice, if using, to
cooking juices and simmer 1 minute. Pour
over mussels and serve.

Makes 2 servings.

— MACKEREL & GOOSEBERRIES —

1 lb. fresh or frozen gooseberries
1 teaspoon fennel seeds
2 (1-lb.) mackerel, each cut into 2 fillets
1 tablespoon olive oil
Salt and freshly ground pepper
1 tablespoon pastis (see Note below)
1 teaspoon sugar
2 tablespoons butter, diced
Parsley sprigs, to garnish

Put gooseberries and fennel seeds in a saucepan with just enough water to cover. Bring to a boil, reduce heat and simmer 7 to 10 minutes or until very soft.

Meanwhile, preheat broiler. With the point of a knife, make three slashes in each mackerel fillet. Season fish, brush with oil on each side and broil 10 minutes, turning once.

Reserve a few gooseberries for garnish. Press remainder through a nylon strainer into a saucepan, pressing hard to extract all the juice. Add pastis, sugar, salt and pepper and heat gently, gradually beating in butter. Pour sauce over fish, garnish with reserved gooseberries and parsley and serve with steamed vegetables.

Makes 4 servings.

Note: Pastis is an anise-flavored liqueur.

—SKATE WITH BROWN BUTTER—

1/3 cup unsalted butter
2 skate wings, each weighing 8 oz.
1 tablespoon chopped fresh parsley
Salt and freshly ground pepper
1 tablespoon fresh lemon juice or white wine vinegar
2 or 3 teaspoons capers
Lemon slices and flat-leaf parsley sprigs, to garnish

Gently heat butter in a small saucepan until foamy. Wring a piece of cheesecloth out in very hot water, use to line a strainer and place over a cup. Pour butter through cheesecloth, to remove white sediment. Pour about half of butter into a large skillet.

Add skate and cook 4 or 5 minutes on each side. Drain on paper towels, then transfer to warmed serving plates. Sprinkle with parsley, salt and pepper and keep warm.

Pour remaining clear butter into a small saucepan and heat until golden brown and nutty smelling. Add lemon juice or vinegar and capers and immediately remove from heat. Pour over skate, garnish with lemon slices and parsley and serve.

Makes 2 servings.

HAKE WITH ORANGE

4 pieces of hake fillet, about 1 inch thick
2/3 cup milk
4 tarragon sprigs
2 tablespoons butter, diced
Salt and freshly ground pepper
1/2 teaspoon finely grated orange zest
1/2 teaspoon finely chopped fresh tarragon
1/4 cup whipping cream
Strips of orange zest, orange slices and tarragon
    sprigs, to garnish

Arrange fish in a single layer in a large skillet. Add milk and lay a tarragon sprig on each piece of fish. Add butter and season with salt and pepper.

Cover with waxed paper and a lid, bring to simmering, then reduce heat and poach gently 8 to 10 minutes or until flesh flakes easily.

Discard tarragon, transfer fish to warmed serving plates, cover and keep warm. Add orange zest and chopped tarragon to pan and boil 2 minutes. Add cream and heat through, simmering for a few minutes if necessary, to thicken sauce. Pour over fish, garnish and serve.

Makes 4 servings.

SOLE MEUNIÈRE

3 tablespoons all-purpose flour
Salt and freshly ground pepper
8 sole fillets, each weighing 3 oz.
3/4 cup unsalted butter
Juice of 2 lemons
2 tablespoons finely chopped fresh parsley
Parsley sprigs and lemon wedges, to garnish

Season flour with salt and pepper. Coat fish lightly and evenly in flour and set aside.

Gently heat 1/2 cup butter in a small saucepan until foamy. Wring a piece of cheesecloth out in very hot water, use to line a strainer and place over a bowl. Carefully skim foam from surface of butter and pour butter through cheesecloth, to remove white sediment.

Heat butter in a large skillet until sizzling. Add fish, in batches, and cook over medium heat 4 minutes on each side, until crisp but not brown. Transfer to warmed serving plates and keep warm. Pour off cooking juices and wipe pan. Add remaining butter to pan and heat until foaming and golden brown. Stir in lemon juice and parsley and immediately pour over fish. Garnish with parsley and lemon and serve.

Makes 4 servings.

── TROUT WITH ALMONDS ──

4 trout, each weighing 10 oz., cleaned
Salt and freshly ground pepper
1/3 cup unsalted butter
1/2 cup sliced almonds
2 tablespoons fresh lemon juice
Dill sprigs and lemon wedges, to garnish

Season trout inside and out with salt and pepper. Heat 1/4 cup of the butter in a large skillet.

Add trout to pan and cook, in batches if necessary, 12 to 15 minutes, turning once, until skin is crisp and flesh flakes easily. Drain trout on paper towels, transfer to warmed serving plates and keep warm.

Wipe pan with paper towels. Heat remaining butter in pan, add almonds and cook, turning occasionally, until lightly browned. Stir in lemon juice, salt and pepper. Quickly pour over fish, garnish with dill and lemon wedges and serve.

Makes 4 servings.

TROUT IN RIESLING

1/4 cup butter, diced
2 tablespoons finely chopped shallot
4 oz. mushrooms, sliced
4 trout, each weighing 10 oz., cleaned
Salt and freshly ground pepper
1-1/4 cups Riesling wine
1/2 cup whipping cream
2 teaspoons finely chopped fresh parsley

Remove heads from trout. Heat 3 tablespoons of the butter in a skillet large enough to hold fish in a single layer, add shallot and mushrooms and cook over low heat, stirring occasionally, 5 minutes or until soft. Lay fish on top and add salt and pepper and wine. Bring just to a simmer, cover and poach fish 10 to 15 minutes or until flesh flakes easily.

Transfer trout to warmed serving plates and keep warm. Boil cooking juices until reduced by half. Reduce heat, add cream and simmer until slightly thickened. Whisk remaining butter into the sauce, one piece at a time. Pour sauce over fish, sprinkle with chopped parsley and serve.

Makes 4 servings.

— BROILED BASS WITH FENNEL —

1 (6-1/2-lb.) bass or bream, cleaned and head
  removed
1 bunch of fennel
Salt and freshly ground pepper
Juice of 1 lemon
3 tablespoons olive oil
Lime slices and fennel sprigs, to garnish

With a sharp knife, cut deep diagonal slashes
in each side of fish and insert a fennel sprig
into each slash.

Preheat broiler or grill. If using broiler, line
broiler pan with foil. Season fish inside and
out with salt and pepper and put 2 or 3
fennel sprigs in cavity. Brush top half of fish
with lemon juice and oil and sprinkle a little
lemon juice and oil inside fish.

Put fish on broiler or grill rack, lay a fennel
sprig on top and cook 8 to 12 minutes or
until top half is cooked and skin is lightly
charred. Turn over carefully, brush with
lemon juice and oil and place another fennel
sprig on top. Cook another 8 to 12 minutes
or until cooked through. Cut into portions,
garnish with lime slices and fennel sprigs and
serve.

Makes 6 servings.

BARBECUED SARDINES

8 sardines, cleaned
6 tablespoons olive oil
3 tablespoons lemon juice
3 tablespoons mixed chopped fresh parsley, basil
  and tarragon
Salt and freshly ground pepper
Basil sprigs, to garnish

Put sardines into a shallow nonmetallic dish. Mix together oil, lemon juice, herbs, salt and pepper and pour over sardines. Cover and refrigerate 2 hours, turning sardines occasionally.

Preheat broiler or grill. Remove sardines from marinade, place on rack and broil 2 or 3 minutes. Turn over, brush with marinade and cook another 3 minutes or until fish flakes easily. Garnish with basil sprigs and serve.

Makes 4 servings.

STUFFED SARDINES

12 sardines, cleaned and heads removed
1 garlic clove, finely chopped
1 tablespoon each chopped fresh chives, fennel,
  parsley and rosemary
1 tablespoon freshly grated Parmesan cheese
1/4 cup almonds, lightly toasted and coarsely
  chopped
2 tablespoons olive oil
Salt and freshly ground pepper
Juice of 1/2 lemon
1/4 cup fresh bread crumbs
Rosemary sprigs, to garnish

Preheat oven to 425F (220C). Oil a wide, shallow roasting pan or ovenproof dish.

Open out sardines and lay, skin side up, on work surface. Press gently with your thumbs along center of back to dislodge backbone. Turn over and gently pull away backbone.

Mix together garlic, herbs, Parmesan cheese, almonds, half the oil, salt and pepper. Lay 6 sardines, skin side down, in a single layer in roasting pan. Sprinkle with lemon juice then spread with herb mixture. Cover with remaining sardines, skin side up. Sprinkle with bread crumbs, then drizzle with remaining oil. Bake 10 minutes or until golden. Garnish with rosemary sprigs and serve hot or at room temperature.

Makes 6 servings.

— SALMON WITH WATERCRESS —

Butter
2 oz. shallots, finely chopped
4 salmon fillets, each weighing 7 oz.
Salt and freshly ground pepper
1 cup dry white wine
1 cup fish stock
4 bunches watercress
1/2 cup whipping cream

Coat a skillet large enough to hold fish in a single layer with a generous covering of butter. Add shallots, lay salmon on top, season with salt and pepper and add wine and stock.

Cover, bring just to a simmer and poach gently about 8 minutes or until fish is opaque and flesh flakes easily. Meanwhile, remove large stalks from watercress and discard. Add watercress to a pan of boiling water and blanch 1 minute. Drain, rinse under cold running water and drain again. Purée in a blender or food processor.

Remove salmon from pan, transfer to warmed serving plates and keep warm. Boil cooking juices rapidly until thickened and reduced to 2/3 cup. Add cream and simmer until thickened to a coating consistency. Add watercress purée and heat gently to warm through. Pour sauce over salmon and serve.

Makes 4 servings.

SALMON IN RED WINE

2 tablespoons unsalted butter
2 salmon steaks, each weighing 6 oz.
2/3 cup red wine such as Chinon or Beaujolais
1 tablespoon chopped fresh tarragon
Salt and freshly ground pepper
Tarragon sprigs, to garnish

Melt half the butter in a skillet, add salmon and cook each side briefly over high heat.

Reduce heat and cook salmon 3 minutes on each side, until salmon is opaque and flesh flakes easily.

Remove salmon from pan, cover and keep warm. Stir wine into pan and boil until reduced by half. Add tarragon, salt and pepper. Dice remaining butter. Remove pan from heat and stir in remaining butter, one piece at a time. Divide sauce among warmed serving plates, place salmon on top, garnish with tarragon sprigs and serve.

Makes 2 servings.

——SCALLOPS IN WHITE WINE——

2 tablespoons unsalted butter
1 tablespoon olive oil
2 shallots, chopped
1 large garlic clove, crushed
1/2 cup dry white wine
1 lb. scallops
1 tablespoon fresh lemon juice
2 tablespoons chopped fresh parsley
Salt and freshly ground pepper
Flat-leaf parsley sprigs, to garnish

Heat butter and oil in a skillet, add shallots and garlic and cook, stirring occasionally, 5 minutes or until soft.

Add wine to pan and boil until reduced by about half. Cut each scallop into 2 or 3 slices, depending on size.

Add scallops to skillet and cook, stirring occasionally, 2 or 3 minutes or until just turning opaque. Stir in lemon juice, parsley, salt and pepper. Garnish with flat-leaf parsley and serve immediately.

Makes 4 servings.

Note: If the scallops still have their coral attached, you can use that too.

— ROAST GARLIC MONKFISH —

1 (2-1/4-lb.) monkfish
1 head of garlic
2 tablespoons olive oil
1/2 teaspoon chopped fresh thyme
1/4 teaspoon fennel seeds
Salt and freshly ground pepper
Juice of 1 lemon
Parsley and thyme sprigs, to garnish

Preheat oven to 425F (220C). Remove all fine skin from fish. Remove center bone, then tie fish firmly back into shape with string. With point of a sharp knife, make a number of small incisions in fish.

Peel 2 garlic cloves and cut into slivers. Insert into incisions in fish. Heat half the oil in a skillet, add fish and cook 5 minutes or until evenly browned on both sides. Transfer to a shallow ovenproof dish and sprinkle with thyme, fennel seeds, salt and pepper.

Add lemon juice and remaining oil. Put remaining garlic, unpeeled, around fish and bake 20 minutes. Garnish with parsley and thyme sprigs and serve with garlic cloves.

Makes 4 servings.

Note: To eat garlic, squeeze flesh from skins and mash into cooking juices.

COQ AU VIN

2 tablespoons butter
2 slices thick-cut smoked bacon, chopped
18 pearl onions
8 oz. button mushrooms
Olive oil for frying (optional)
6 chicken legs
1 onion, chopped
1 carrot, diced
2 garlic cloves, crushed
1-1/2 tablespoons all-purpose flour
2-1/2 cups red Burgundy wine
3/4 cup chicken stock
Bouquet garni
Salt and freshly ground pepper
Chopped fresh parsley, to garnish

Melt butter in a heavy Dutch oven, add bacon and cook until crisp. Remove with a slotted spoon and drain on paper towels. Add pearl onions to pan and cook, stirring occasionally, until golden. Remove with a slotted spoon and drain on paper towels. Add mushrooms to pan, adding oil if necessary, and cook until lightly browned. Remove with a slotted spoon and drain on paper towels. Add chicken to pan and cook over medium to high heat until browned all over. Remove and drain on paper towels.

Add chopped onion and carrot to pan and cook until lightly browned, adding garlic towards end of cooking. Add flour and cook, stirring, 2 minutes. Stir in wine and stock and bring to a boil. Return all ingredients to pan, add bouquet garni, salt and pepper, cover and cook over very low heat 50 to 60 minutes. Remove chicken and vegetables, discard bouquet garni and boil sauce to thicken. Return chicken and vegetables to pan. Garnish with parsley and serve.

Makes 6 servings.

— CHICKEN WITH TARRAGON —

2 tablespoons finely chopped fresh tarragon
1/4 cup butter, softened
1 (3-1/2-lb.) chicken
Salt and freshly ground pepper
1/2 cup dry white wine
1/4 cup whipping cream
Tarragon sprigs, to garnish

Preheat oven to 400F (205C). Beat tarragon into butter, then push butter between chicken breast and skin.

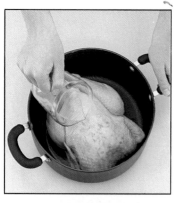

Season chicken with salt and pepper and put in a heavy Dutch oven. Add wine. Cover tightly and cook in oven 30 minutes. Reduce oven temperature to 350F (180C) and cook 1-1/4 to 1-1/2 hours or until chicken is tender.

Transfer chicken to a warmed plate and keep warm. Tilt pan and spoon off the fat, leaving behind cooking juices. Boil cooking juices to thicken to a light sauce. Reduce heat, stir in cream and simmer to thicken slightly. Carve chicken, garnish with tarragon sprigs and serve with sauce.

Makes 4 servings.

– CHICKEN WITH MUSHROOMS –

1 tablespoon olive oil
1 tablespoon unsalted butter, diced
4 chicken quarters
12 oz. chestnut, oyster, shiitake or chanterelle
   mushrooms, or a mixture
1 onion, finely chopped
3/4 cup Vouvray or similar fruity, medium-dry white
   wine
2 tablespoons chopped fresh tarragon leaves
1/2 cup regular plain yogurt
Salt and freshly ground pepper
Tarragon sprigs, to garnish

Heat oil and butter in a heavy Dutch oven, add chicken and cook until browned. Remove with a slotted spoon.

Preheat oven to 325F (165C). Cut large mushrooms into quarters and oyster mushrooms into 1-inch strips. Add to pan with onion and cook, stirring occasionally, 5 minutes or until soft. Stir in wine and bring to a boil. Return chicken to pan and sprinkle with tarragon. Cover tightly and cook in the oven 1 hour.

Using a slotted spoon, transfer chicken and vegetables to a warmed plate and keep warm. Boil cooking liquid to thicken slightly. Stir in yogurt and reheat gently without boiling. Season with salt and pepper. Return chicken and vegetables to pan, turn in sauce and heat gently to warm through. Garnish with tarragon sprigs and serve.

Makes 4 servings.

— CHICKEN IN CREAM SAUCE —

4 slices thick-cut bacon, diced
1 tablespoon butter
1 small onion, chopped
4 boneless chicken breasts
1 lb. celeriac, chopped
1 bay leaf
1 cup dry white wine or chicken stock
2/3 cup crème fraîche or whipping cream
Salt and freshly ground pepper

Heat a Dutch oven over medium heat, add bacon and cook until fat runs. Remove with a slotted spoon and set aside.

Melt butter in pan, add onion and cook, stirring occasionally, 2 or 3 minutes. Add chicken and celeriac and cook, stirring occasionally and turning chicken once or twice, 5 minutes. Add bacon, bay leaf, wine or stock, and enough water to cover. Bring to a boil, reduce heat, cover and simmer 30 minutes or until chicken is tender.

Remove the chicken, bacon and vegetables with a slotted spoon, transfer to a warmed plate and keep warm. Boil cooking liquid to thicken slightly. Discard bay leaf, stir in crème fraîche or cream, return to a boil, reduce heat and simmer 3 or 4 minutes. Return chicken, bacon and vegetables to pan, season with salt and pepper and heat gently to warm through. Serve hot.

Makes 4 servings.

BURGUNDY CHICKEN

2 tablespoons butter
4 chicken legs
1 shallot, finely chopped
2 tablespoons marc de Bourgogne or brandy
1 cup white Burgundy or other Chardonnay wine
2 thyme sprigs
Salt and freshly ground pepper
8 oz. seedless green grapes, halved
1/4 cup crème fraîche or whipping cream
Flat-leaf parsley and thyme sprigs, to garnish

Melt butter in a heavy Dutch oven, add chicken and cook until browned all over. Remove and drain on paper towels.

Add shallot to pan and cook, stirring occasionally, 2 or 3 minutes or until soft. Return chicken to pan. Add marc de Bourgogne or brandy and set alight. When flames have died down, add wine, thyme, salt and pepper.

Bring to a boil, reduce heat, cover and simmer, turning chicken two or three times, 50 to 60 minutes. Transfer chicken to warmed serving plates and keep warm. Add grapes to pan and boil until sauce is slightly thickened. Stir in crème fraîche or cream and simmer to thicken slightly. Pour over chicken, garnish with flat-leaf parsley and thyme and serve.

Makes 4 servings.

POULET PROVENÇAL

10 garlic cloves
1 tablespoon finely chopped fresh thyme
1 tablespoon finely chopped fresh marjoram
Salt and freshly ground pepper
1 (3-1/2-lb.) chicken, cut into 8 pieces
2 tablespoons fresh lemon juice
1/4 cup olive oil
1 thyme sprig
1 small rosemary sprig
6 basil leaves, shredded
8 anchovy fillets, drained and chopped
4 beefsteak tomatoes, peeled, seeded and chopped
2/3 cup dry white wine
24 Niçoise olives
Chopped fresh herbs and basil sprigs, to garnish

Crush 2 garlic cloves and mix with chopped herbs and a small pinch of salt. Cut small incisions in chicken and insert a little herb mixture into each incision. Rub with lemon juice and pepper and refrigerate 2 hours. Preheat oven to 325F (165C). Heat half the oil in a saucepan. Finely chop remaining garlic and add to pan with thyme, rosemary and basil. Cook, stirring occasionally, 5 minutes. Stir in anchovy fillets, tomatoes, wine and pepper. Bring to a boil, reduce heat and simmer 15 minutes.

Heat remaining oil in a heavy Dutch oven, add chicken and cook until browned all over. Add sauce, cover and cook in the oven 45 minutes, turning chicken once or twice. Add olives and cook 15 minutes. Garnish with mixed herbs and basil sprigs and serve.

Makes 4 servings.

Note: Niçoise olives have a special flavor as they are marinated in oil and herbs. If you can't get them, use plain ripe olives instead.

POULET BASQUAISE

3 red bell peppers
1 (3-lb.) chicken, cut into 8 pieces
Salt and freshly ground pepper
3 tablespoons olive oil
2 onions, thinly sliced
3 garlic cloves, chopped
1/2 fresh red chile, cored, seeded and chopped
4 beefsteak tomatoes, peeled, seeded and chopped
Bouquet garni
4 oz. Bayonne ham or prosciutto, diced
1/2 cup dry white wine
Chopped fresh parsley, to garnish

Preheat broiler. Broil bell peppers, until charred and blistered all over.

Leave bell peppers until cool enough to handle, then peel. Halve, remove cores and seeds and cut flesh into strips. Season chicken with salt and pepper. Heat oil in a heavy Dutch oven, add chicken and cook until browned all over. Remove with tongs or a slotted spoon, transfer to a large plate and set aside.

Add onions and garlic to pan and cook, stirring occasionally, 5 minutes or until soft. Stir in chile, tomatoes and bouquet garni and simmer 15 minutes. Stir in ham, wine and bell peppers. Bring to a boil, add chicken and any juices on plate and season with pepper. Cover tightly and simmer 50 to 60 minutes or until tender. Transfer chicken to warmed serving plates. Boil sauce to thicken, pour over chicken, garnish with chopped parsley and serve.

Makes 4 servings.

LEMON CHICKEN

1/4 cup butter
1 (3-1/2-lb.) chicken, quartered
16 pearl onions
1 cup chicken stock
1 cup dry white wine
Bouquet garni
Salt and freshly ground pepper
12 button mushrooms, quartered
2 large egg yolks, lightly beaten
Juice of 1/2 lemon
Chopped fresh parsley, to garnish

Melt butter in a heavy Dutch oven, add chicken pieces and onions and cook 10 minutes or until chicken is browned.

Remove onions with a slotted spoon and set aside. Add stock, wine, bouquet garni, salt and pepper. Bring to a boil, reduce heat, cover and simmer 20 minutes. Return onions to pan and cook 20 minutes. Add mushrooms and cook 10 minutes.

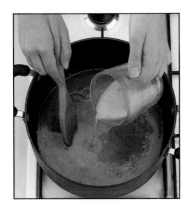

Using a slotted spoon, transfer chicken and vegetables to a warmed dish, cover and keep warm. Boil cooking liquid until reduced by one-third. Remove a ladleful of cooking liquid, allow to cool slightly, then stir into egg yolks. Reduce heat, stir egg yolk mixture into pan and heat very gently, stirring, until slightly thickened; do not boil. Stir in lemon juice. Return chicken and vegetables to pan and turn in sauce. Garnish with parsley and serve.

Makes 4 servings.

BRAISED CHICKEN

1 (3-1/2-lb.) chicken
1 onion, halved
2 whole cloves
2 slices bacon, chopped (optional)
About 4-1/2 cups stock or water
Bouquet garni
Salt and freshly ground pepper
4 stalks celery, quartered
4 carrots, quartered
4 small turnips, quartered
12 small leeks, halved
Bay leaves, to garnish

Put chicken into a large heavy Dutch oven. Stud each onion half with 1 clove.

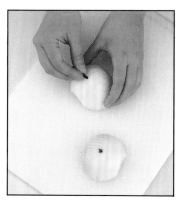

Add onion halves to pan with bacon, if using. Add enough stock or water to cover and bring to a boil. Add bouquet garni, salt and pepper. Skim scum from surface, cover and simmer 1 hour.

Add celery, carrots and turnips, cover and cook 30 minutes. Add leeks and cook 15 minutes or until chicken and vegetables are tender. Transfer chicken and vegetables to a warmed serving plate and keep warm. Boil sauce to thicken slightly. Carve chicken and serve with the vegetables and sauce, garnished with bay leaves.

Makes 4 servings.

CHICKEN CHASSEUR

1 tablespoon olive oil
3 tablespoons butter
4 chicken quarters
3 shallots, finely chopped
1 garlic clove, finely chopped
1 tablespoon all-purpose flour
5 oz. brown or shiitake mushrooms, sliced
1 cup dry white wine
2 beefsteak tomatoes, peeled, seeded and chopped
Several tarragon and parsley sprigs
Salt and freshly ground pepper
Tarragon sprigs, to garnish

Heat oil and 2 tablespoons of the butter in a heavy Dutch oven, add chicken and cook until browned all over.

Remove chicken and set aside. Add shallots and garlic to pan and cook, stirring occasionally, 5 minutes or until soft. Add flour and mushrooms and cook, stirring, until flour has browned lightly. Stir in wine and tomatoes. Bring to a boil, stirring.

Return chicken to pan and add herbs, salt and pepper. Cover tightly and cook over low heat 50 to 60 minutes. Remove chicken with a slotted spoon, transfer to warmed plates and keep warm. Remove herbs from sauce and discard. Boil sauce to thicken slightly. Reduce heat and stir in remaining butter. Pour sauce over chicken, garnish with tarragon sprigs and serve.

Makes 4 servings.

POULET AU VINAIGRE

1 tablespoon vegetable oil
1 tablespoon butter
4 chicken legs
1 onion, finely chopped
Bouquet garni
4 tomatoes, peeled, seeded and chopped
2 teaspoons tomato paste
1-1/4 cups red wine vinegar
1-1/4 cups chicken stock
Salt and freshly ground pepper
Chopped fresh parsley, to garnish

Heat oil and butter in a heavy Dutch oven. Add chicken and cook until lightly browned all over.

Remove chicken and set aside. Add onion to pan and cook, stirring occasionally, 5 minutes or until soft. Return chicken to pan, add bouquet garni, cover and cook over low heat 20 minutes, turning occasionally.

Add tomatoes to pan, and cook, uncovered, until liquid has evaporated. Combine tomato paste and vinegar and add to pan. Simmer until most of liquid has evaporated. Add stock, salt and pepper and simmer until reduced by half. Sprinkle with parsley and serve.

Makes 4 servings.

GARLIC CHICKEN

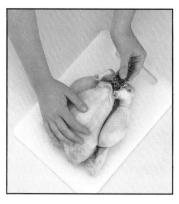

1 bunch of thyme
1 (3-1/2-lb.) chicken
2 heads of garlic, separated into cloves but not
    peeled
Salt and freshly ground pepper
3/4 cup dry white wine
1 tablespoon butter, diced
Thyme sprigs, to garnish

Preheat oven to 400F (205C). Put some thyme sprigs into cavity of chicken. Put chicken into a heavy Dutch oven just large enough to hold chicken, and tuck remaining thyme sprigs and a few cloves of garlic around it.

Add remaining garlic cloves and wine. Season chicken with salt and pepper. Bring to a boil, cover tightly and cook in the oven 30 minutes. Reduce oven temperature to 350F (180C) and cook 1-1/4 to 1-1/2 hours or until chicken is very tender.

Transfer chicken and garlic to a warmed serving plate and keep warm. Discard thyme. Tilt pan and spoon off fat, leaving behind cooking juices. Boil cooking juices to thicken slightly. Remove from heat and stir in butter. Carve chicken, garnish with thyme sprigs and serve with garlic cloves and sauce.

Makes 4 servings.

Note: Garlic cooked in this way has a mild, sweet flavor. To eat, squeeze cloves out of skin and mash into sauce.

DUCK WITH ORANGE

2 boneless duck breasts, each weighing 6 oz.
Salt and freshly ground pepper
1-1/2 teaspoons chopped fresh thyme
2 oranges
1 teaspoon cornstarch
Juice of 1 lemon
1/4 cup Cointreau
1 tablespoon unsalted butter
Orange twists and thyme sprigs, to garnish

Using a sharp knife, score skin and fat on duck breasts in a crisscross pattern, taking care not to cut through flesh. Season with salt and pepper and rub with thyme.

Heat a heavy skillet over medium to high heat, add duck, skin side down, and cook 10 to 12 minutes, reducing heat a little if skin becomes too brown. Turn duck over and cook 5 minutes, or to taste. Transfer duck to a warmed plate and keep warm.

Meanwhile, remove 1-1/2 tablespoons zest from oranges. Add to a small pan of boiling water and blanch 2 minutes. Drain, rinse in cold water and set aside. Squeeze juice from oranges. Pour most of fat from skillet. Stir cornstarch into pan, then add orange and lemon juice and orange zest. Bring to a boil, stirring, then add Cointreau, salt and pepper. Reduce heat and whisk in butter. Slice duck, arrange on serving plates, add sauce, garnish and serve.

Makes 2 servings.

DUCK WITH TURNIPS

1 (4- or 5-lb.) duck
Salt and freshly ground pepper
1 tablespoon olive oil
1 cup chicken stock
1/2 cup dry white wine
Bouquet garni
1-1/4 lbs. small turnips, halved or quartered
Pinch of sugar
Sage sprigs, to garnish

Season duck generously inside and out with salt and pepper and prick fatty areas of breasts with a fork.

Heat oil in a heavy Dutch oven, add duck and cook over low heat, turning, until browned all over. Pour fat from pan, reserving 2 tablespoons. Add stock, wine and bouquet garni to pan, cover tightly and cook over low heat 30 minutes.

Meanwhile, heat reserved duck fat in a skillet, add turnips, sprinkle with sugar and cook until browned all over. Add turnips to pan, baste with cooking liquid and cook, uncovered, 25 minutes or until duck and turnips are tender. Transfer duck and turnips to a warmed serving plate. Skim fat from sauce, then boil sauce to thicken slightly. Season with salt and pepper and remove bouquet garni. Carve duck, garnish and serve with turnips and sauce.

Makes 4 servings.

BOEUF BOURGUIGNON

1 or 2 tablespoons olive oil
2 slices thick-cut bacon, chopped
12 each pearl onions and button mushrooms
2 lbs. beef chuck steak, cubed
1 large onion, finely chopped
1 carrot, finely chopped
3 garlic cloves, chopped
1 tablespoon all-purpose flour
3 cups red Burgundy wine
Bouquet garni
Salt and freshly ground pepper
Chopped fresh parsley, parsley sprigs and bay
  leaves, to garnish

Heat 1 tablespoon oil in a heavy Dutch oven,
add bacon and cook 2 or 3 minutes.

Remove with a slotted spoon and set aside.
Add pearl onions to pan and cook, stirring
occasionally, until browned. Remove with a
slotted spoon and set aside. Add mushrooms
to pan and cook, stirring occasionally, until
lightly browned, adding more oil if needed.
Remove with a slotted spoon and set aside.
Add beef to pan and cook over medium to
high heat until browned all over. Remove
with a slotted spoon and set aside.

Add chopped onion and carrot to pan and
cook, stirring occasionally, until beginning to
brown. Return bacon and beef to pan, add
garlic and stir in flour. Stir in wine, bouquet
garni, salt and plenty of pepper. Heat until
almost simmering, cover and cook over very
low heat 2-3/4 hours, stirring occasionally.
Add reserved onions and mushrooms, cover
and cook 10 minutes, to warm through.
Garnish with parsley and bay leaves and
serve.

Makes 4 servings.

– BOEUF EN DAUBE PROVENÇAL –

2-1/4 lbs. beef chuck steak, cubed
1 Spanish onion, chopped
3 garlic cloves, chopped
Bouquet garni
1 teaspoon black peppercorns
3 cups full-bodied red wine
2 tablespoons olive oil
8 oz. bacon, cut into strips
3 tomatoes, peeled, seeded and chopped
2-inch-wide strip orange peel, oven-dried
Salt and freshly ground pepper
12 black olives
Flat-leaf parsley, to garnish

Put steak, onion, garlic, bouquet garni, peppercorns and wine in a nonmetallic bowl.

Cover and refrigerate 12 to 24 hours. Preheat oven to 325F (165C). Remove meat from marinade with a slotted spoon, reserving marinade, and drain beef on paper towels. Heat oil in a heavy Dutch oven, add bacon and cook until browned. Remove with a slotted spoon and set aside. Add beef and cook over medium to high heat until browned all over. Add tomatoes and cook 2 or 3 minutes.

Add reserved marinade, bacon and orange peel and season with salt and pepper. Heat until almost simmering, cover tightly and cook in oven 3-1/4 hours or until beef is very tender. Add olives and cook 15 minutes. Discard bouquet garni and orange peel, garnish with parsley and serve.

Makes 4 to 6 servings.

Note: To dry orange peel, put in a very low oven and leave until hard.

ENTRECÔTE BORDELAISE

7 oz. bone marrow (optional)
1/4 cup butter
2 oz. shallots, finely chopped
3/4 cup red Bordeaux wine
Bouquet garni
1 tablespoon olive oil
1 lb. piece boneless beef sirloin steak
Salt and freshly ground pepper
1 tablespoon chopped fresh parsley

Put marrow, if using, in a saucepan, add enough water to cover and bring to a boil. Remove from heat and set aside. Heat half the butter in a saucepan, add shallots and cook, stirring occasionally, 3 to 5 minutes.

Add wine and bouquet garni, bring to a boil and boil until reduced by half. Meanwhile, heat oil in a skillet, add steak and fry 2 to 4 minutes on each side, according to taste. Transfer to a warmed plate, season and keep warm. Remove bouquet garni from sauce and season sauce with salt and pepper. Reduce heat and whisk in remaining butter.

Cut steak diagonally into 4 thick slices. Drain marrow, cut diagonally into 4 slices and add to sauce. Pour sauce over steak, sprinkle with parsley and serve immediately.

Makes 2 servings.

- STEAK WITH BÉARNAISE SAUCE -

4 beef sirloin steaks, about 1-inch thick
Salt and freshly ground pepper
BÉARNAISE SAUCE:
1/2 cup unsalted butter, diced
3 stalks each tarragon and chervil
2 teaspoons chopped shallot
4 black peppercorns, crushed
2 tablespoons dry white wine
2 tablespoons white wine vinegar
2 egg yolks
1 teaspoon each chopped fresh tarragon, parsley and
   chervil

Preheat broiler. Oil broiler rack, add steaks
and season with pepper.

Broil 1 to 3 minutes on each side, according
to taste. Meanwhile, make sauce. Melt butter
in a small saucepan. Put tarragon and chervil
stalks, shallot, peppercorns, wine and vinegar
in a small saucepan, bring to a boil and boil
until reduced to 2 teaspoons. Strain.

Put egg yolks into a blender or food
processor with 2 teaspoons water and
process briefly to combine. With motor
running at low speed, pour in reduced liquid.
With motor still running at low speed, pour
in melted butter in a slow, steady stream, to
make a thick sauce. Add herbs, salt and
pepper and serve immediately with steaks.

Makes 4 servings.

Note: Use only very fresh, uncracked eggs
for sauce.

—— CARBONNADE DE BOEUF ——

2 tablespoons olive oil
2 lbs. beef chuck steak, cubed
1 lb. onions, sliced
2 tablespoons all-purpose flour
2-1/2 cups brown ale
1 garlic clove, crushed
Bouquet garni
4 thick slices French bread
Salt and freshly ground pepper
Dijon mustard
Flat-leaf parsley and chopped fresh parsley, to
  garnish

Heat oil in a heavy Dutch oven, add meat and cook until browned all over. Remove with a slotted spoon and set aside.

Add onions to pan and cook over low heat, stirring occasionally, 10 minutes or until browned. Sprinkle with flour and cook, stirring, until lightly browned. Stir in beer and bring to a boil, stirring. Return beef to pan, add garlic and bouquet garni, cover tightly and cook over very low heat 2 hours or until meat is tender, stirring occasionally.

Preheat broiler to low. Toast bread slowly until crisp and golden. Spread thickly with mustard, baste lightly with sauce from pan and toast 5 to 10 minutes or until topping is browned. Garnish stew with parsley and serve with toasted bread.

Makes 4 servings.

NAVARIN OF LAMB

1 tablespoon olive oil
2-1/4 lbs. boneless lamb, cubed
1 onion and 1 large carrot, finely chopped
Pinch of sugar
2 teaspoons all-purpose flour
1/2 cup dry white wine
2-1/2 cups veal or chicken stock
Bouquet garni
Salt and freshly ground pepper
3 tomatoes, peeled, seeded and chopped
3 small turnips, quartered
12 pearl onions
12 small new potatoes
12 baby carrots, halved or quartered
5 oz. shelled fresh green peas (about 1 cup)
Parsley sprigs, to garnish

Heat oil in a heavy Dutch oven, add lamb and cook until browned all over. Remove with a slotted spoon and set aside. Add chopped onion and carrot and cook, stirring occasionally, 10 minutes or until browned. Sprinkle with sugar and flour and cook, stirring, until lightly browned. Add wine, stock, bouquet garni, salt and pepper. Add tomatoes and bring to a boil, stirring. Return lamb to pan, cover tightly and cook over low heat 30 minutes.

Add turnips, onions and potatoes, cover and cook 20 minutes. Add baby carrots and cook 10 minutes. Add peas and cook 5 to 7 minutes or until lamb and vegetables are tender. Remove lamb and vegetables with a slotted spoon, transfer to a warmed bowl and keep warm. Boil cooking juices to thicken slightly. Return lamb and vegetables to pan and turn in sauce. Garnish with parsley and serve.

Makes 4 servings.

LAMB BOULANGÈRE

1 (4-1/2-lb.) leg of lamb
4 garlic cloves
Salt and freshly ground pepper
3 tablespoons butter
2 lbs. potatoes, thickly sliced
1 Spanish onion, thinly sliced
1 bay leaf
2 thyme sprigs
About 1-1/4 cups veal or vegetable stock or water
1 tablespoon olive oil
Flat-leaf parsley, to garnish

Cut small incisions in lamb. Thinly slice 2 of the garlic cloves and insert into incisions.

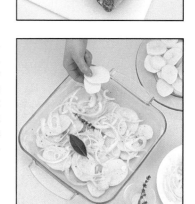

Season lamb with salt and pepper; set aside. Preheat oven to 325F (165C). Use 1 tablespoon of the butter to coat a shallow baking dish. Crush remaining garlic. Arrange layers of potatoes, onion, garlic, herbs, salt and pepper in the buttered dish. Add enough stock or water to just cover, dot with remaining butter, cover with foil and bake 1 hour.

Heat oil in a heavy skillet, add lamb and cook quickly until lightly browned all over. Put lamb on top of potatoes and cover with foil. Increase oven temperature to 375F (190C) and bake lamb and potatoes 1-1/4 to 1-1/2 hours, uncovering 15 minutes before end, to brown. Carve lamb, garnish with flat-leaf parsley and serve with potatoes.

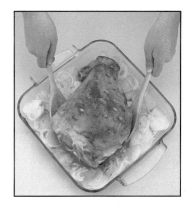

Makes 6 servings.

LAMB & FLAGEOLET BEANS

4 lamb shanks, each weighing 8 oz.
4 garlic cloves, thinly sliced
2 tablespoons olive oil
1 onion, finely chopped
1-1/2 cups dried flageolet beans, soaked overnight
1-1/4 lbs. tomatoes, peeled, seeded and chopped
1 tablespoon tomato paste
2/3 cup red wine
Bouquet garni
Salt and freshly ground pepper
1 small bunch of parsley, chopped
Flat-leaf parsley and bay leaves, to garnish

Cut 4 incisions in each lamb shank. Insert a slice of garlic in each incision.

Heat oil in a heavy Dutch oven, add shanks and cook until browned all over. Remove and set aside. Add onion and remaining garlic to pan and cook, stirring occasionally, 5 minutes or until soft but not browned.

Drain and rinse beans and add to pan with tomatoes, tomato paste, wine, bouquet garni, salt and pepper. Return lamb to pan, cover tightly and cook over low heat 1-1/2 to 2 hours or until lamb and beans are tender. Discard bouquet garni and stir in parsley. Garnish and serve with béarnaise sauce (see page 74).

Makes 4 servings.

LAMB WITH ROSEMARY

1 (4-1/2-lb.) leg young lamb
3 rosemary sprigs
2 or 3 garlic cloves, cut into slivers
Salt and freshly ground pepper
1/4 cup butter
2/3 cup red or white wine

Preheat oven to 450F (230C). Cut small incisions in lamb with the point of a sharp knife.

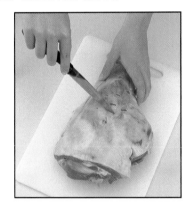

Remove leaves from one of rosemary sprigs. Insert leaves and garlic slivers into incisions. Season lamb with salt and pepper, put the remaining rosemary sprigs on top and dot with butter. Put into a roasting pan and roast 15 minutes. Reduce oven temperature to 350F (180C) and roast another 40 to 60 minutes or to desired doneness.

Leave lamb in oven, with door propped open, 15 minutes, to rest. Remove lamb from roasting pan and transfer to a serving plate. Tilt roasting pan and spoon off most of fat. Add wine, stirring to release browned bits. Bring to a boil over medium heat, reduce heat and simmer briefly. Season with salt and pepper. Carve lamb, garnish with rosemary sprigs and serve with sauce.

Makes 6 servings.

─ TARRAGON LAMB NOISETTES ─

1 tablespoon olive oil
1/4 cup butter
8 boneless lamb chops, about 1-inch thick
Salt and freshly ground pepper
1/4 cup brandy
3 tablespoons whipping cream
2 tablespoons chopped fresh tarragon
Tarragon sprigs and flat-leaf parsley, to garnish

Heat oil and half the butter in a heavy skillet until sizzling.

Add lamb and cook 2-1/2 or 3 minutes on each side, until well-browned but still pink in the center. Remove with tongs, transfer to warmed serving plates, season with salt and pepper and keep warm.

Add remaining butter to pan. When melted, add brandy, stirring to release browned bits, and bring to a boil. Stir in cream and tarragon and boil until thickened. Season with salt and pepper, pour over lamb, garnish with tarragon sprigs and flat-leaf parsley and serve.

Makes 4 servings.

KIDNEYS IN RED WINE

3 tablespoons butter
3 shallots, finely chopped
1 garlic clove, finely chopped
1/2 cup red wine
3 tablespoons water
Bouquet garni
Salt and freshly ground pepper
1 tablespoon olive oil
1 lb. lamb kidneys, halved and cored
2 teaspoons Dijon mustard
2 tablespoons whipping cream
Flat-leaf parsley and chopped parsley, to garnish

Heat 2 tablespoons of the butter in a saucepan, add shallots and garlic and cook, stirring occasionally, 3 minutes or until soft.

Add wine, water, bouquet garni, salt and pepper. Bring to a boil, reduce heat and simmer 5 minutes. Discard bouquet garni. Meanwhile, heat oil and remaining butter in a large skillet, add kidneys and cook, stirring, over medium to high heat 3 or 4 minutes or until kidneys are cooked through. Remove with a slotted spoon and keep warm.

Stir wine sauce, mustard and cream into skillet, stirring to release browned bits. Add kidneys, together with any juices on plate, and heat through gently: do not boil. Garnish with parsley and serve.

Makes 3 or 4 servings.

—— RABBIT WITH MUSTARD ——

1/3 cup butter
3-1/2 lbs. boneless rabbit portions
Salt and freshly ground pepper
1/4 cup Dijon mustard
1 cup fresh bread crumbs
1 tablespoon chopped fresh tarragon
Tarragon sprigs, to garnish

Heat 1/4 cup of the butter in a large skillet. Add rabbit and cook until lightly browned all over.

Season rabbit with salt and pepper. Remove with tongs, transfer to a wire rack and leave 10 minutes. Preheat oven to 475F (240C). Grease a roasting pan. Spread mustard over rabbit portions, then coat in bread crumbs. Arrange rabbit in roasting pan in a single layer and bake 20 minutes.

Transfer rabbit portions to a warmed dish and keep warm. Melt remaining butter and pour over rabbit. Sprinkle with chopped tarragon, garnish with tarragon sprigs and serve.

Makes 4 servings.

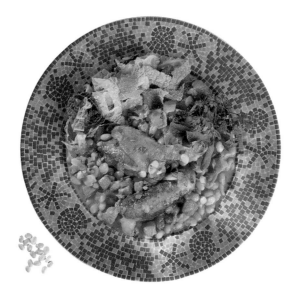

CASSOULET

1-1/2 cups dried haricot beans, soaked overnight
2 tablespoons olive oil
4 slices thick-cut smoked bacon, chopped
6 pork sausages
3 duck legs, halved
2 large onions, chopped
2 garlic cloves, crushed
12 oz. tomatoes, peeled and chopped
1-1/2 tablespoons tomato paste
1/2 cup dry white wine
Large bunch of fresh herbs
Salt and freshly ground pepper
Fresh herbs and chopped fresh parsley, to garnish

Drain and rinse beans. Put into a saucepan, cover with cold water and bring to a boil.

Boil rapidly 10 minutes, reduce heat, cover and simmer 50 minutes or until just tender. Drain beans, reserving 1 cup cooking liquid. Preheat oven to 325F (165C). Heat oil in a large Dutch oven, add bacon and sausages and cook until lightly browned. Remove with a slotted spoon and drain on paper towels. Add duck portions to pan and cook until lightly browned. Remove and drain on paper towels.

Add onions to pan and cook, stirring occasionally, 7 minutes or until beginning to color. Return meats to pan with beans, reserved cooking liquid and remaining ingredients except garnish. Bring to a boil, cover and bake 1 to 1-1/4 hours or until beans and duck are tender, uncovering towards end of cooking to thicken juices. Garnish with herbs and parsley and serve.

Makes 6 servings.

MARINATED SPICED PORK

1 tablespoon olive oil
1 (3-1/2-lb.) boneless pork leg, skin and fat removed
4 oz. brown or shiitake mushrooms, sliced
Thyme sprigs and celery leaves, to garnish
Salt
MARINADE:
2 tablespoons olive oil
1 onion, finely chopped
1 carrot, finely chopped
1 stalk celery, chopped
2 cups full-bodied red wine
6 juniper berries, crushed
8 black peppercorns, crushed
1/4 teaspoon ground allspice
Bouquet garni

To make marinade, heat oil in a heavy skillet, add onion and carrot and cook, stirring occasionally, 5 minutes. Add celery and cook, stirring occasionally, until vegetables are browned. Add wine, juniper berries, peppercorns, allspice, bouquet garni and salt. Let cool. Put pork into a nonmetallic dish, add marinade, cover and refrigerate 24 hours, turning occasionally. Preheat oven to 350F (180C). Remove pork and vegetables with a slotted spoon, drain pork on paper towels and reserve vegetables. Strain marinade and set aside.

Heat oil in a heavy Dutch oven just large enough to hold pork, add pork and cook until browned all over. Remove and set aside. Add mushrooms and cook 5 minutes. Add reserved vegetables and put pork on top. Add marinade. Heat until almost simmering, cover and cook in oven, turning occasionally, 2 to 2-1/2 hours or until pork is tender. Transfer to a warmed plate. Skim fat from sauce, then boil to thicken. Season with salt. Carve pork, garnish and serve with sauce.

Makes 4 to 6 servings.

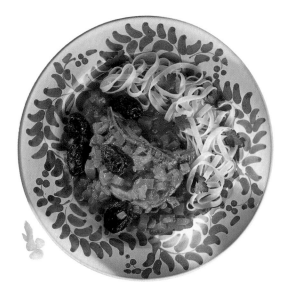

PORK WITH PRUNES

5 oz. large pitted prunes
2-1/2 cups dry white wine
3 tablespoons butter
4 pork chops
1 each onion, carrot and celery, chopped
1 cup veal or pork stock
Bouquet garni
Salt and freshly ground pepper
Squeeze of lemon juice

Combine prunes and half the wine in a bowl; let soak overnight.

Heat 2 tablespoons of the butter in a heavy Dutch oven, add chops and cook quickly until browned on both sides. Remove and set aside. Add vegetables to pan and cook, stirring occasionally, 5 to 7 minutes or until lightly browned. Stir in remaining wine, bring to a boil and boil 2 or 3 minutes. Add stock and bring to a boil. Return chops to pan, add bouquet garni, salt and pepper, cover tightly and cook over low heat 45 minutes.

Add prunes and soaking liquid to pan, bring to a boil, cover and cook 30 minutes or until pork is tender. Transfer pork and prunes to warmed serving plates and keep warm. Discard bouquet garni and boil sauce to thicken slightly. Reduce heat and gradually stir in remaining butter. Add lemon juice to taste, pour sauce over pork and prunes and serve.

Makes 4 servings.

PORK WITH CIDER

2 tablespoons butter
4 pork chops
1 onion, finely chopped
2 teaspoons Calvados or brandy
1-1/4 cups unsweetened apple juice
1 bay leaf
Salt and freshly ground pepper
2 small cooking apples, peeled, cored and sliced
1 tablespoon fresh lemon juice
2 tablespoons crème fraîche or sour cream
Salt and freshly ground pepper
Thyme sprigs and leaves, to garnish

Melt butter in a heavy Dutch oven, add chops and cook quickly until browned on both sides. Remove and set aside.

Preheat oven to 350F (180C). Add onion to pan and cook, stirring occasionally, 5 minutes or until soft. Add Calvados or brandy and set alight. When flames die down, stir in apple juice and bring to a boil. Return chops to pan, add bay leaf, salt and pepper, cover tightly and bake 20 minutes.

Toss apples in lemon juice. Add to pan, cover again and cook 10 to 15 minutes or until pork and apples are tender. Remove pork and apples from pan with a slotted spoon, transfer to warmed plates and keep warm. Boil cooking liquid until lightly syrupy. Stir in crème fraîche or sour cream, pour over pork and apples, garnish with thyme and serve.

Makes 4 servings.

POIS À LA FRANÇAISE

1/4 cup butter
3 green onions, white parts only, finely chopped
1 small iceberg lettuce, coarsely chopped
1 lb. shelled fresh or frozen green peas
2 parsley sprigs
1-1/2 teaspoons chopped fresh mint
Pinch of sugar (optional)
Salt and freshly ground pepper
Mint sprigs, to garnish

Heat half the butter in a large saucepan, add green onions and lettuce and cook, stirring, 2 minutes.

Add peas, herbs, sugar if using, salt and pepper. Add enough water to just cover and bring to a boil. Reduce heat, cover and simmer 12 to 20 minutes, depending on age of peas, until peas are tender.

Drain peas and transfer to a warmed serving dish. Stir in remaining butter, garnish with mint sprigs and serve.

Makes 4 servings.

CAROTTES VICHY

1 lb. young carrots, thinly sliced diagonally
Salt
2 tablespoons unsalted butter
2 teaspoons sugar
1 tablespoon finely chopped fresh chervil or parsley
Chervil sprigs, to garnish

Put carrots into a heavy saucepan and add enough water to just cover. Add a little salt.

Bring to a boil, reduce heat and simmer, uncovered, stirring occasionally, until carrots are tender and nearly all the water has evaporated.

Add butter and sugar and cook, shaking pan frequently, until carrots are lightly coated with glaze. Sprinkle with chervil or parsley, garnish with chervil sprigs and serve.

Makes 4 servings.

POTATOES FORESTIÈRE

12 oz. mixed mushrooms
1 lb. potatoes
Leaves from a bunch of parsley or basil
4 garlic cloves, crushed
Salt and freshly ground pepper
Flat-leaf parsley sprigs and basil leaves, to garnish

Preheat oven to 350F (180C). Thinly slice mushrooms and potatoes.

Generously oil a baking dish that will hold potatoes and mushrooms in a layer no more than 1-1/2 inches deep. In a large bowl, toss together mushrooms, potatoes, parsley or basil, garlic, salt and pepper.

Spread potato mixture in dish in an even layer and bake about 45 minutes or until potatoes are tender, turning mixture halfway through. Let stand a few minutes before serving. Garnish with flat-leaf parsley and basil and serve.

Makes 4 servings.

— GLAZED CARROTS & ONIONS —

8 oz. baby carrots
8 oz. pearl onions
2 tablespoons butter
1-1/2 tablespoons sugar
Salt and freshly ground pepper
2 tablespoons brown veal stock or juices from
    roasted meat (optional)
Chopped fresh parsley, to garnish

Put carrots and onions into a heavy saucepan with half the butter, 1 tablespoon of the sugar and 1-1/4 cups water.

Bring to a boil, reduce heat and simmer, uncovered, stirring occasionally, until carrots and onions are tender and water has evaporated.

Add remaining butter and sugar, salt, pepper and stock or roasting juices, if using. Increase heat slightly and cook, shaking pan occasionally, until vegetables are coated with glaze and beginning to brown. Garnish with chopped parsley and serve.

Makes 4 servings.

— BROAD BEANS WITH SAVORY —

1 lb. shelled broad beans or lima beans
Few sprigs summer savory
2 tablespoons butter
1 egg yolk
2/3 cup crème fraîche or sour cream
Salt and freshly ground pepper
Carrot ribbons and chervil sprigs, to garnish

Put beans and some of the savory sprigs in a saucepan of boiling salted water and cook about 25 minutes or until tender. Drain.

Melt butter in a saucepan over low heat. Finely chop remaining savory and add to saucepan with beans.

Mix egg yolk with crème fraîche or sour cream. Stir into beans and cook over low heat, stirring, until sauce thickens; do not boil. Season with salt and pepper. Garnish with carrot ribbons and chervil sprigs and serve.

Makes 4 servings.

— FENNEL & PARMESAN GRATIN —

4 small fennel bulbs
3 tablespoons fresh lemon juice
1/4 cup unsalted butter
1 tablespoon olive oil
1/2 cup freshly grated Parmesan cheese
Salt and freshly ground pepper
1/4 cup sliced almonds, toasted

Trim feathery fronds from fennel and reserve. Cut fennel lengthwise into quarters.

Add fennel and lemon juice to a saucepan of boiling salted water and cook 15 minutes or until fennel is tender but still crisp. Drain, place on paper towels and drain thoroughly.

Preheat oven to 400F (205C). Arrange fennel in a single layer in a baking dish, dot with butter, drizzle with olive oil, sprinkle with cheese and season with plenty of pepper. Bake, uncovered, 20 to 25 minutes or until golden. Sprinkle with toasted almonds, garnish with reserved fennel fronds and serve.

Makes 4 servings.

ZUCCHINI GRATIN

2 lbs. zucchini, sliced
1/3 cup butter
1 lb. tomatoes, peeled, seeded and chopped
2 garlic cloves, chopped
2 tablespoons chopped fresh basil or parsley
Salt and freshly ground pepper
1 cup fresh bread crumbs
4 or 5 tablespoons finely grated Gruyère cheese
Basil sprigs, to garnish

Put zucchini into a colander, sprinkle generously with salt and leave 1 hour. Rinse well, drain and dry thoroughly with paper towels.

Preheat oven to 400F (205C). Heat 1/4 cup of the butter in a skillet, add zucchini and cook, stirring occasionally, 7 minutes or until browned. Remove with a slotted spoon and set aside.

Add tomatoes, garlic, basil or parsley, salt and pepper to skillet, bring to a boil, reduce heat and simmer until thickened. Stir in zucchini. Turn into a shallow baking dish. Mix together bread crumbs and cheese and sprinkle over zucchini. Dot with remaining butter and bake 25 minutes. Garnish with basil sprigs and serve.

Makes 4 to 6 servings.

GRATIN SAVOYARD

2 lbs. potatoes
1-1/2 cups shredded Gruyère cheese
Freshly grated nutmeg
Salt and freshly ground pepper
About 1 cup chicken or vegetable stock
1/4 cup butter
Flat-leaf parsley sprigs, to garnish

Slice potatoes very thinly, keeping them in a bowl of cold water before slicing. Preheat oven to 400F (205C).

Grease a shallow baking dish. Layer potatoes in dish, sprinkling each layer with cheese, nutmeg, salt and pepper, and finishing with a layer of cheese.

Add enough stock to come almost to the top of potatoes. Dot with butter. Bake 10 minutes. Reduce oven temperature to 350F (180C) and bake 50 minutes or until potatoes are tender and top is golden, and adding more stock if potatoes start to become dry. Garnish with parsley and serve.

Makes 4 servings.

— WARM GOAT CHEESE SALAD —

2 tablespoons olive oil
2 tablespoons walnut or hazelnut oil
1 teaspoon black peppercorns, coarsely crushed
1 tablespoon chopped fresh thyme
4 goats cheeses or 4 slices goat cheese
8 oz. frisée or other small leaf lettuce
1 oz. arugula
4 thin slices French bread
1 tablespoon red wine vinegar
1/2 teaspoon Dijon mustard

Mix together oils, peppercorns and thyme.
Put cheese into a small shallow dish and add
oil mixture.

Turn cheese in oil, to coat, and refrigerate 12
to 14 hours, turning cheese occasionally.
Preheat broiler. Arrange lettuce and arugula
on serving plates. Remove cheese from oil,
reserving oil.

Brush both sides of each slice of bread with a
little reserved oil. Toast one side of bread.
Turn over, top with cheese and broil under a
very high heat until cheese is beginning to
brown. Whisk together vinegar and mustard
then slowly whisk in reserved oil. Pour
dressing over salad greens, top with the
broiled goat cheese and serve immediately.

Makes 4 servings.

ROQUEFORT SALAD

1/2 cup walnut pieces
2 bunches watercress
4 oz. Roquefort cheese
DRESSING:
1 tablespoon red wine vinegar
1/2 to 1 teaspoon Dijon mustard
1/4 cup olive oil
Salt and freshly ground pepper

To make dressing, whisk together vinegar and mustard, then slowly pour in oil, whisking constantly. Season with salt and pepper and set aside.

Preheat broiler. Spread walnut pieces on a baking sheet and broil, turning occasionally, until crisp and evenly browned.

Put watercress into a serving bowl, crumble Roquefort cheese over watercress and sprinkle with toasted walnuts. Whisk dressing, pour over salad, toss and serve.

Makes 4 servings.

CHICKPEA SALAD

1-1/2 cups dried chickpeas, soaked overnight
1 tablespoon finely chopped fresh parsley
1-1/2 teaspoons finely chopped fresh tarragon
4 green onions, finely chopped
Sliced green onion and flat-leaf parsley, to garnish
DRESSING:
2 garlic cloves, finely chopped
1 tablespoon red wine vinegar
2 or 3 teaspoons Dijon mustard
Salt and freshly ground pepper
1/4 cup olive oil

Drain and rinse chickpeas. Put into a saucepan and cover with cold water.

Bring to a boil. Reduce heat, cover and simmer 1 to 1-1/2 hours or until chickpeas are tender. Meanwhile, make dressing. Mix together garlic, vinegar, mustard, salt and pepper. Slowly pour in oil, whisking constantly.

Drain chickpeas and immediately toss with dressing, parsley, tarragon and green onions. Garnish with green onion slices and flat-leaf parsley and serve warm.

Makes 4 servings.

WARM SPINACH SALAD

1 lb. small spinach leaves
6 slices thick-cut lean bacon, cut into strips
2 slices bread, crusts removed
1/4 cup olive oil
4 teaspoons red wine vinegar
1 teaspoon Dijon mustard
Salt and freshly ground pepper

Put spinach into a serving bowl. Heat a nonstick skillet, add bacon and cook until crisp and brown. Remove with a slotted spoon and drain on paper towels. Drain off fat from skillet.

Cut bread into cubes. Add 1 tablespoon of the oil to skillet, add bread and fry over medium to high heat until crisp and golden. Remove and drain on paper towels. Add to spinach with bacon.

Stir vinegar and mustard into skillet and bring to a boil. Add remaining oil, salt and pepper. Heat through and pour over salad. Toss and serve immediately.

Makes 4 servings.

POTATO SALAD

1-1/2 lbs. small new potatoes
4 or 5 mint leaves, chopped
1 tablespoon chopped fresh chives
1/2 shallot, finely chopped
Mint sprigs, to garnish
DRESSING:
1 tablespoon wine vinegar
2 teaspoons Dijon mustard
Salt and freshly ground pepper
3 tablespoons olive oil

Cook potatoes in a saucepan of boiling salted water 15 minutes or until tender.

Meanwhile, make dressing. Whisk together vinegar, mustard, salt and pepper. Slowly pour in oil, whisking constantly.

Drain potatoes thoroughly, cut into halves or quarters, depending on size, then immediately toss with dressing, herbs and shallot. Let cool. Garnish with mint sprigs and serve.

Makes 4 servings.

SALADE NIÇOISE

8 oz. small green beans
1 head lettuce
4 beefsteak tomatoes, cut into wedges
1 red bell pepper, chopped
3 hard-cooked eggs, quartered
1 (7-oz.) can tuna in olive oil, drained
Leaves from small bunch of flat-leaf parsley,
    coarsely chopped
16 pitted ripe olives
6 to 8 anchovy fillets, halved lengthwise
DRESSING:
1/2 cup olive oil
2 teaspoons wine vinegar
1 or 2 garlic cloves, crushed
Salt and freshly ground pepper

Cut beans crosswise in halves and cook in a saucepan of boiling salted water 10 minutes or until tender. Drain, rinse in cold water and drain again. Let cool. Tear lettuce into bite-size pieces and arrange on a large serving plate with beans, tomatoes, bell pepper, eggs and tuna.

Sprinkle with parsley and olives. Arrange anchovies on top in a lattice pattern. To make dressing, whisk together olive oil, vinegar, garlic, salt and pepper. Pour over salad and serve.

Makes 4 servings.

BRAISED LENTILS

1 tablespoon olive oil
2 slices lean thick-cut bacon, cut into strips
1 onion, chopped
1 carrot, diced
2 garlic cloves, finely chopped
1-1/4 cups green or brown lentils
Bouquet garni
1 (14-oz.) can crushed tomatoes
Salt and freshly ground pepper
Flat-leaf parsley, to garnish

Heat oil in a large saucepan, add bacon and cook until lightly browned. Remove with a slotted spoon and drain on paper towels.

Add onion and carrot to pan and cook, stirring occasionally, 7 minutes. Add garlic and cook 2 or 3 minutes or until vegetables are lightly browned. Stir in lentils and mix well. Return bacon to pan and add bouquet garni. Pour in enough water to cover by 1 inch and bring to a boil.

Cover and simmer 20 to 25 minutes or until lentils are almost tender and most of liquid has evaporated. Add more water during cooking if necessary. Drain lentils, discarding bouquet garni, and return to pan. Add tomatoes, salt and pepper and simmer 10 minutes. Garnish with flat-leaf parsley and serve.

Makes 4 servings.

STUFFED CABBAGE LEAVES

1 Savoy cabbage
2 lbs. chestnuts
1/4 cup butter
4 oz. lean ground pork
1 onion, finely chopped
2 stalks celery, finely chopped
1/2 cup fresh bread crumbs
2 eggs, lightly beaten
2-1/2 tablespoons chopped fresh parsley
Grated zest of 1 lemon
Salt and freshly ground pepper
6 slices prosciutto
Basil leaves, to garnish
TOMATO & MUSHROOM SAUCE:
2 tablespoons olive oil
1 onion, finely chopped
1 garlic clove, chopped
4 oz. mushrooms, sliced
1-1/2 lbs. tomatoes, peeled, seeded and chopped
1 tablespoon tomato paste
Bouquet garni

Remove 12 large leaves from cabbage. Blanch in boiling water 1 minute. Remove with a slotted spoon and drain well. Cut out center ribs. Add remaining whole cabbage to pan and cook 4 minutes. Drain thoroughly. Cut in half, cut out core and shred leaves, discarding any thick ribs.

Cut a slit in each chestnut. Add to a saucepan of boiling water and cook 10 minutes. Removing a few chestnuts from pan at a time, peel off outer and inner skins while still hot. Cook peeled chestnuts in a fresh pan of boiling water about 20 minutes or until tender. Drain and coarsely chop.

Melt butter in a large skillet, add shredded cabbage and cook, stirring occasionally, 7 or 8 minutes or until tender. Remove with a slotted spoon and transfer to a large bowl. Add pork, onion and celery to pan and cook, stirring occasionally, until pork is browned. Add to cabbage with chestnuts, bread crumbs, eggs, parsley, lemon zest, salt and pepper.

Line a small bowl with a piece of cheesecloth. Put two blanched cabbage leaves into bowl then cover with a slice of ham. Add one-sixth of stuffing. Gather up ends of cloth and tie with string to make a tight ball. Repeat with remaining ingredients to make six balls. Add to a large pan of boiling water, weight down with a plate and simmer 30 minutes.

Meanwhile, make sauce. Heat oil in a saucepan, add onion and cook 3 minutes. Stir in garlic, mushrooms, tomatoes, tomato paste, bouquet garni, salt and pepper. Simmer 10 minutes or until thickened. Discard bouquet garni. Lift stuffed cabbage from pan, drain well, then unwrap and turn out onto warmed serving plates. Add sauce, garnish with basil leaves and serve.

Makes 6 servings.

RATATOUILLE

2 eggplant, sliced
3 zucchini, sliced
3 or 4 tablespoons olive oil
1 Spanish onion, very thinly sliced
3 garlic cloves, crushed
2 large red bell peppers, thinly sliced
4 ripe beefsteak tomatoes, peeled, seeded and
  chopped
Leaves from a few sprigs of thyme, marjoram and
  oregano
Salt and freshly ground pepper
2 tablespoons each chopped fresh parsley and basil

Put eggplant and zucchini in a colander, sprinkle generously with salt and let stand 1 hour.

Rinse well, drain and dry thoroughly with paper towels. Heat 2 tablespoons of the oil in a heavy Dutch oven, add eggplant and cook, stirring occasionally, a few minutes. Add 1 tablespoon more oil, onion and garlic and cook, stirring occasionally, 2 minutes. Add bell peppers and cook, stirring occasionally, 2 minutes.

Add zucchini to pan with more oil if necessary. Cook, stirring occasionally, 2 or 3 minutes, then add tomatoes, thyme, marjoram and oregano. Season lightly with salt and pepper, cover and cook over very low heat 30 to 40 minutes, stirring occasionally. Stir in parsley and basil and cook, uncovered, 5 to 10 minutes or until liquid has evaporated. Serve warm or cold.

Makes 4 servings.

CLAFOUTIS

1-1/2 lbs. sweet cherries, pitted
3 eggs
1/4 teaspoon almond extract
3 tablespoons sugar, plus extra for sprinkling
3 tablespoons all-purpose flour
2 cups milk
2 tablespoons butter
Mint sprigs, to decorate

Preheat oven to 425F (220C). Butter a large shallow baking dish and add cherries to dish.

Mix together eggs, almond extract, 3 tablespoons sugar and flour. Put milk into a saucepan, bring almost to a boil and stir into egg mixture.

Pour egg mixture over cherries, dot with butter and bake 20 to 25 minutes or until just set and lightly browned. Cut into squares, sprinkle with sugar, decorate with mint and serve warm.

Makes 4 servings.

COEURS À LA CRÈME

2 cups fromage frais or 1 cup cream cheese and 1
   cup sour cream
1 cup whipping cream
3 egg whites
Mint sprigs, to decorate
Sugar or vanilla sugar and fresh fruit, to serve

Line 6 individual coeurs à la crème molds
with pieces of cheesecloth.

In a large bowl, beat fromage frais or cheese
and sour cream until smooth, then whisk in
cream. Whisk egg whites until stiff. Fold into
cheese mixture. Spoon into molds, put
molds in a roasting pan or on a baking sheet
and leave in the refrigerator 12 to 24 hours,
to drain. The longer the mixture is left, the
firmer it becomes.

Turn molds onto chilled plates. Decorate
with mint sprigs and serve with sugar or
vanilla sugar and fresh fruit.

Makes 6 servings.

Variation: Whip whipping cream until soft
peaks form. Fold into fromage frais. Omit
beaten egg whites.

Note: To make vanilla sugar, simply store a
vanilla bean in a jar of sugar, so that it
absorbs the flavor.

CRÈME CARAMEL

2-1/2 cups milk
1 vanilla bean
2 eggs
2 egg yolks
1/3 cup sugar
Mint sprigs, to decorate
CARAMEL:
1/2 cup sugar
5 tablespoons water

To make caramel, put sugar and water into a small heavy saucepan and heat gently until sugar has dissolved. Increase heat and boil until golden brown.

Remove from heat and carefully pour into 6 (2/3-cup) ramekins, turning dishes to coat sides with caramel. Put into a roasting pan and let cool. Preheat oven to 325F (165C). Put milk and vanilla bean into a small saucepan and bring almost to a boil. Cover, remove from heat and let stand 20 minutes. Whisk together eggs, egg yolks and sugar in a large bowl. Remove vanilla bean from milk and return milk almost to a boil. Stir into egg mixture.

Strain milk mixture into ramekins. Pour boiling water into roasting pan to come halfway up sides of ramekins and bake 40 to 50 minutes or until lightly set. Remove from pan, cool and refrigerate until needed. One hour before serving, run knife around edge of desserts and turn out onto serving plates. Decorate with mint and serve.

Makes 6 servings.

— PETITS POTS AU CHOCOLAT —

2-1/2 cups half-and-half or milk
1 vanilla bean
Butter for greasing
1 egg
5 egg yolks
3 tablespoons sugar
8 oz. semisweet chocolate, chopped
1 tablespoon instant coffee granules
Whipped cream and chocolate shavings, to decorate

Put half-and-half or milk and vanilla bean into a small saucepan and bring almost to a boil over low heat. Cover, remove from heat and let stand 15 minutes.

Preheat oven to 300F (150C). Butter 6 to 8 custard cups or ramekins and put into a roasting pan. Whisk together egg, egg yolks and sugar in a large bowl until thick and pale. Remove vanilla bean from half-and-half and return half-and-half almost to a boil.

Remove half-and-half from heat, add chocolate and coffee and stir until dissolved. Stir into egg mixture. Strain into cups, pour boiling water into pan to come halfway up sides of cups and bake about 1 hour, until very lightly set. Transfer cups to a wire rack and let cool. Chill. Decorate with whipped cream and chocolate shavings and serve.

Makes 6 to 8 servings.

OEUFS À LA NEIGE

3 eggs, separated
1/2 cup sugar
2 egg yolks
2 cups milk
1-1/2 to 2 tablespoons Cointreau, orange flower
  water or rose water
Strips of orange zest and mint sprigs, to decorate

Bring a large skillet of water to a boil. Meanwhile, whisk egg whites until stiff but not dry. Gradually whisk in half the sugar until mixture is stiff and shiny.

Reduce heat beneath pan so water is barely simmering. Float spoonfuls of egg white onto water, a few at a time so they are not crowded, and poach 2 or 3 minutes, turning halfway through. Remove with a slotted spoon, transfer to a tilted tray and leave to drain. Whisk all 5 egg yolks with remaining sugar until thick and pale. Put milk into a saucepan and bring almost to a boil.

Stir a little milk into egg yolk mixture then, over low heat, stir back into milk. Cook over low heat, stirring, until slightly thickened; do not boil. Let cool, stirring occasionally. Refrigerate if not serving immediately. Just before serving, add Cointreau or flower water and pour custard into shallow serving bowls. Float meringues on top, decorate with orange zest and mint and serve.

Makes 4 to 6 servings.

BRETON PRUNE PUDDING

7 oz. pitted prunes
1/4 cup rum or hot water
2 tablespoons butter
1/2 cup all-purpose flour
About 3 tablespoons granulated sugar
4 eggs, beaten
2 cups milk
Powdered sugar, for dusting
Lemon wedges and mint sprigs, to decorate

Put prunes into a bowl, add rum or hot water and let stand 2 hours. Put butter into a shallow baking dish and put in oven while preheating it to 400F (205C).

Combine flour and sugar in a bowl. Gradually stir in eggs and then milk, to make a smooth batter. Drain liquid from prunes and add liquid to batter.

Put prunes into baking dish, carefully add batter around prunes and bake about 1 hour, until puffed, just set in center and golden brown on top. Let cool slightly. Cut into squares and dust with powdered sugar. Decorate with lemon wedges and mint sprigs and serve warm.

Makes 4 servings.

PEARS IN RED WINE

4 firm pears, peeled, with stalks left on
4 whole cloves
8 pitted prunes
2-1/2 cups red wine
1 or 2 tablespoons sugar
1-1/2 cinnamon sticks
1 vanilla bean
2 tablespoons crème de cassis
Orange slices and bay leaves, to decorate

Preheat oven to 250F (120C). Insert 1 clove into each pear and put into a Dutch oven with prunes.

Put wine, sugar, cinnamon sticks and vanilla into a saucepan and bring to a boil over low heat, stirring until sugar has dissolved. Pour over pears, cover and bake 3 hours, turning and basting pears twice.

Transfer pears and prunes to a serving dish, standing pears upright. Remove vanilla bean. Add cassis to cooking liquid and boil rapidly until lightly syrupy. Add sauce and let cool. Refrigerate before serving. Slice pears and arrange on serving plates. Decorate with orange slices and bay leaves and serve.

Makes 4 servings.

PEACHES IN WHITE WINE

4 peaches
4 raspberries, strawberries or small pieces of almond
  paste
1 or 2 tablespoons sugar, preferably vanilla flavored
  (page 106)
1-1/4 cups fruity white wine, chilled
Lemon twists, raspberries and raspberry leaves, to
  decorate

Put peaches into a large bowl, cover with boiling water and leave about 20 seconds. Remove peaches from water, peel, then cut in half and remove pits.

Put a raspberry, strawberry or piece of almond paste in cavity of each peach and reassemble peaches. Put peaches into four serving dishes, sprinkle with sugar and add wine. Cover and refrigerate until chilled, turning peaches once. Decorate and serve.

Makes 4 servings.

──SUMMER FRUIT GRATIN──

2 large peaches, peeled and sliced
1/2 cup raspberries
3/4 cup sliced strawberries
About 1/3 cup red currants and blueberries or black
   currants
2 tablespoons kirsch or Cointreau (optional)
2 tablespoons granulated sugar
1-1/4 cups crème fraîche or whipping cream
1/2 cup packed light brown sugar

Divide fruit among four heatproof serving
dishes. Sprinkle with kirsch or Cointreau, if
using, and granulated sugar.

Whip crème fraîche or cream until it forms
soft peaks. Spread over fruit and refrigerate
at least 1 hour.

Preheat broiler to very hot. Sprinkle a thick
even layer of brown sugar over crème fraîche
or cream. Broil until sugar is bubbling and
caramelized. Serve immediately.

Makes 4 servings.

TARTE AU CITRON

3 eggs
1 egg yolk
3/4 cup granulated sugar
Grated zest and juice of 3 lemons
Grated zest and juice of 1 orange
1/2 cup powdered sugar, plus extra for dusting
Shredded zest of 1 lemon
Lemon twists and chervil sprigs, to decorate
PÂTE SUCRÉE:
3/4 cup all-purpose flour
Pinch of salt
1/4 cup sugar
1/2 cup unsalted butter, softened
2 egg yolks

To make pâte sucrée, sift flour and salt onto a marble slab or a work surface and make a well in center. Put sugar, butter and egg yolks into well and pinch them together to form a paste, then lightly draw in flour, adding about 1 tablespoon cold water to make a soft but firm dough. Cover and refrigerate 2 hours.

Roll out pastry on a lightly floured surface and use to line a 9-1/2-inch loose-bottomed fluted tart pan, pressing pastry well into sides and bottom. Run rolling pin over top of pan to cut off excess pastry. Refrigerate 20 minutes. Preheat oven to 400F (205C).

Prick bottom of pastry case with a fork, line with waxed paper or foil and fill with dried beans. Put tart pan on a baking sheet and bake 10 to 12 minutes. Reduce oven temperature to 375F (190C). Remove paper and beans and bake 5 minutes or until golden. Transfer pan to a wire rack and let cool. Leave oven on.

Mix together eggs, egg yolk, granulated sugar and grated lemon and orange zests and juices. Return tart pan to baking sheet and ladle in filling. Bake 25 to 30 minutes or until set. Transfer pan to a wire rack, cool slightly, then remove outer ring of tart pan. Leave tart to cool completely.

Put powdered sugar and 2/3 cup water in a small pan and heat gently, stirring, until dissolved. Boil 2 minutes, then add shredded lemon zest and simmer until shiny. Remove with a slotted spoon and let cool on waxed paper. Just before serving, dust tart thickly with sifted powdered sugar and sprinkle with candied lemon zest. Garnish with lemon twists and chervil sprigs and serve with cream, if desired.

Makes 6 to 8 servings.

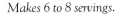

TARTE TATIN

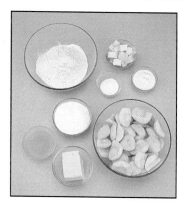

1/2 cup unsalted butter, softened
1/2 cup sugar
About 3 lbs. firm, well-flavored apples, peeled,
    cored and cut into wedges
Juice of 1 lemon
Strips of lemon zest and mint sprigs, to decorate
PASTRY:
2 cups all-purpose flour
1 tablespoon sugar
1/2 cup butter, diced
2 or 3 tablespoons crème fraîche

To make pastry, combine flour and sugar in a
bowl. Add butter and rub or cut in until
mixture resembles fine bread crumbs. Add
enough crème fraîche to form a dough. Form
into a ball, cover and refrigerate at least 30
minutes.

Spread butter over bottom of a heavy 9-1/2-
inch cake pan or ovenproof skillet. Sprinkle
with sugar and arrange apples on top,
rounded-side down.

Sprinkle with lemon juice and cook over medium to high heat, shaking pan occasionally, 20 to 30 minutes or until apples are lightly caramelized. If a lot of juice is produced, pour it off into a saucepan, boil to a thick syrup and pour back over apples.

Preheat oven to 425F (220C). Roll out pastry on a lightly floured surface until slightly larger than pan. Lay pastry on top of apples, tucking edge of pastry down side of pan.

Prick pastry lightly with a fork and put pan on a baking sheet. Bake 20 minutes or until pastry is golden. Turn tart onto a warmed serving plate, decorate with lemon zest and mint sprigs and serve.

Makes 6 to 8 servings.

Note: Be careful when turning out the tart as the syrup will be very hot and can burn.

RED FRUIT TART

9-1/2-inch loose-bottomed fluted tart pan lined with
 pâte sucrée (page 114)
About 26 each raspberries, halved strawberries and
 pitted cherries
3 tablespoons red fruit jam
1 tablespoon fresh lemon juice
Raspberries and raspberry leaves, to decorate
CRÈME PÂTISSIÈRE:
2/3 cup milk
2/3 cup half-and-half
1 vanilla bean
3 egg yolks
1/4 cup sugar
1 tablespoon all-purpose flour
1-1/2 tablespoons cornstarch
1 tablespoon unsalted butter

To make crème pâtissière, place milk, half-
and-half and vanilla bean into a saucepan and
heat gently to simmering point. Remove
from heat, cover and leave 30 minutes.
Whisk egg yolks and sugar until pale and
very thick. Stir in flour and cornstarch.
Remove vanilla bean from milk and return
almost to a boil. Slowly whisk into egg
mixture. Return to pan and bring to a boil,
whisking. Simmer 2 or 3 minutes. Remove
from heat, stir in butter and pour into a
bowl. Let cool, stirring occasionally. Cover
and refrigerate. Preheat oven to 400F (205C).

Prick pastry case with a fork, line with waxed
paper or foil and fill with dried beans. Bake
10 to 12 minutes. Reduce oven temperature
to 375F (190C). Remove paper and beans and
bake 8 to 10 minutes. Cool on a wire rack.
Fill pastry case with crème pâtissière and
arrange fruit on top. Put jam and lemon juice
in a pan and heat gently, to soften. Strain and
brush over fruit. Let cool, decorate and
serve.

Makes 6 servings.

MADELEINES

3 eggs, separated
1/2 cup granulated sugar
1 cup all-purpose flour, plus extra for dusting
1 teaspoon baking powder
1/2 cup unsalted butter, melted
1-1/2 tablespoons fresh lemon juice
Grated zest of 1 large lemon
Powdered sugar for dusting
Strips of lemon zest, chervil sprigs and fresh fruit, to
  decorate

Whisk together egg yolks and granulated sugar until thick and pale yellow. Sift flour and baking powder over mixture.

Using a large metal spoon, fold in flour and baking powder, slowly pouring in butter and lemon juice at same time. Whisk egg whites until stiff but not dry. Fold egg whites and lemon zest into egg yolk mixture. Cover and refrigerate 30 minutes. Preheat oven to 425F (220C). Generously butter madeleine molds and dust with flour.

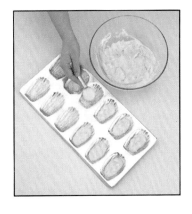

Spoon mixture into molds so they are no more than two-thirds full. Bake 7 minutes or until puffed. Reduce oven temperature to 375F (190C) and bake another 7 minutes or until pale gold on top and slightly darker around edges. Remove from molds, transfer to a wire rack and dust with powdered sugar. Decorate and serve warm.

Makes 20.

Note: The madeleines can be baked in batches, if necessary.

INDEX